ISBN 978-0-265-79306-0
PIBN 10890215

This book is a reproduction of an important historical work. Forgotten Books uses
state-of-the-art technology to digitally reconstruct the work, preserving the original format
whilst repairing imperfections present in the aged copy. In rare cases, an imperfection in
the original, such as a blemish or missing page, may be replicated in our edition. We do,
however, repair the vast majority of imperfections successfully; any imperfections that
remain are intentionally left to preserve the state of such historical works.

FALL
1919

SPRING
1920

# *BLUE GRASS NURSERIES*

*H. F. Hillenmeyer & Sons*   *LEXINGTON, KY.*

# *Foreword*

The Agricultural activity after the war has been felt by nurserymen also, and today there are booked and contracted for more trees and plants than ever in the history of our business. All seem to be vitally interested in the permanent improvement of their properties by planting both fruits and ornamentals.

This unusual demand, following as it does several years of necessary restrictions, unsettled labor and other depressing conditions, will tend to make our products command higher prices. That there is a real shortage of many varieties existing today, is very evident and for this reason we must ask some liberties of substitution when we are out of varieties offered. With this situation existing, patrons wishing certain varieties will do well in ordering early.

## An Appreciation

To those who have favored us with their good patronage this past and previous years, we here wish most heartily to thank you. We trust our business association has been mutually pleasant and that we will merit a continuance of that patronage extended our firm from year to year. We feel that the failure to express this appreciation and thanks, would leave a debt unpaid.

## An Introduction

To those not familiar with the personnel, reputation or practices of this firm, we pause a moment to explain. This finds us entering into the 78th year of nursery practice. Three generations represent this cycle of horticultural activity. From the pack-saddled grafts and cuttings borne overland from the East and European sources, planted by our grandfather, grew the first trees offered by a Kentuckian in 1841. His small production was readily sold and gave birth to the present establishment greatly broadened through the passing years. Today the same practices that have made the name Hillenmeyer almost a household word in the state are continued, and the success achieved by our predecessors is an incentive to its younger blood.

## Policies

**AGENTS.** Most emphatically is it stated that we have **No Agents.** Too many persons are tricked by the transient tree sellers, who operate in a section for a short period and disappear. With them goes the little assurance had of any satisfactory adjustment when their stock, which all too often, proves valueless. Our catalog omits purposely any of these paper made descriptions of super-productive and extra hardy varieties, gigantic sized fruits, pedigree grown trees, other fads and fancies, offered at inflated prices that later prove ordinary or worthless. Our stock is mostly grown here, varieties offered are tested and proven valuable. Our prices are made direct to the planter—published the same to all, in our catalog, a rule to which we must adhere. This enables us to sell at moderate prices, handle our trees without undue exposure and therefore they are more likely to live.

**GUARANTY.** All the stock we sell is more or less of a perishable nature, and therefore we cannot guarantee it to grow—Delay in transit, improper care after receiving, injudicious planting, impoverished or unadapted soils and subsequent care and weather conditions are all beyond our actual control. Any one or a combination of these circumstances may cause a tree to die, regardless of the vigor and vitality

it possesses when shipped. If the stock sent you is not received in good condition, we earnestly advise you to report at once, as any adjustment or correction must be made promptly in order to ascertain the real cause of such complaint. When we deliver and have signed for in good condition to the transportation company, our responsibility as to the physical condition of the stock ceases. **If there is a case of mislabeling, we will, on proper proof, replace such trees with ones of the correct variety or refund the original purchase price. We assume no responsibility beyond this, and all orders are understood to bear this guarantee only.**

**TERMS.** Our firm is responsible—our prices are reasonable and every plant offered is correctly quoted in our catalog—and with existing business conditions we ask everyone to remit with the order. We will ship C. O. D. all orders not paid for in advance—this not being a matter of your credit but we do it with all, regardless of their rating. If for any reason credit is extended, a charge for packing such orders is made. This includes materials and time.

**SERVICE.** We offer our patrons the benefit of our experience in growing, caretaking, planting or suggestions covering the products we sell. Under the various headings throughout the catalog we give some cultural directions covering that particular variety but further offer our assistance to any patron desiring it.

**LOCATION.** To those intending to visit our nurseries we are 3 miles north of Lexington. Take Georgetown Road (Dixie Highway) or trolley to Station 7. Passing a branch nursery on this cross road you will come to our offices, warehouse and packing plant. Visitors welcome.

**DATE OF SHIPMENT.** The fall season usually opens in late October or very early November. This depends on weather conditions—frost being necessary to ripen the wood buds before digging can be done. The spring season opens in March—after danger of all severe weather damage has passed.

**RESPONSIBILITY.** Any prospective patron, wishing to inquire as to our integrity and responsibility is referred to any bank, business house, resident of our city or in central Kentucky, or either commercial agency.

**IN ORDERING—Parcel Post.** A great many plants may be sent by parcel post. The approximate postage for the first zone—150 miles radius from Lexington — is mentioned under their respective prices. No trees can be sent except very small ones owing to postal regulations. In all cases postage must accompany order. Use the order blank, write your name plainly so as to avoid confusion and mistakes.

# Orchard and Garden Possibilities

The planting of fruit trees bespeaks thrift. A little ordinary care for a few years and not necessarily expert attention will result in quick maturing trees and a very enviable harvest of fruit. For the space occupied we know of nothing more profitable on the average place than fruit. Many plant unsuited varieties; others allow the weeds or disease to take their trees; some never plant, and all invariably get the same result. A few fruit trees in the garden, or back yard will do well if you haven't space for an orchard. Peach and cherry especially require little space in a town lot, plums thrive better in the chicken runs or grapes trained on the fences or buildings are all producers under fair attention. Plant well developed trees from reliable sources, care for them as you do other crops and you will realize your dream in good fruit. Our efforts for seventy-eight years have been to produce these trees—our results have been, thousands of bearing orchards of the right kind throughout the state.

The home orchard should be planted near the dwelling on good soil, sloping, preferably to the north or west. Soil not robbed of its fertility, properly tilled and in physical condition to receive a grain crop will produce much better results than orchards set in impoverished fields, in post holes and no further attention given.

Between the rows of the orchard, low growing crops of vegetables and berries may be planted without losing use of land, and at the same time increasing the maturity of the trees by constant cultivation. Green manure crops, of rye, clover, soy beans or cow peas may be plowed under to further enrich the soil.

In the selection of varieties choose those that are dependable and plant a succession from June to late fall. Plant the early varieties in smaller numbers and closer to the home—the winter sorts in greater quantity to facilitate storage or sales. Between the permanent trees in order to economize space, quick maturing or "fillers" may be planted. Peach and plum are largely used besides some apple varieties. When in doubt of what to plant, any open orders sent will have our personal attention and a succession of fruit will be arranged for your requirements. You are always at liberty to inquire of us for any information desired. The increasing cost of growing, of materials and the inability to get stock from abroad on which to work our varieties will cause an increase in price from year to year and we suggest to those contemplating an orchard to plant now.

For the Home Garden. We can supply a complete assortment of Raspberries and Blackberries, Gooseberries and Currants, as well as Asparagus, Rhubarb, Sage or Horseradish.

We have growing for spring sales only, strawberries, which at this writing bid fair to produce us a million plants. Second crop seed potatoes, grown and specially selected for a number of years will be offered in our spring catalog. A copy of this is to be mailed to every patron within the year, and to any others interested, we suggest that you file your name for our spring mailing list.

Proper distances to plant follow—depending on the character and fertility of your soil.

| | Feet each way |
|---|---|
| Apples | 30 to 40 |
| Peaches, Pears, Plums and Cherries | 18 to 20 |
| Grapes | 8 x 8 |
| Currants, Gooseberries, Rhubarb | 4 x 3 |
| Raspberries | 5 x 3 |
| Blackberries | 7 x 3 |

## How to Plant

When trees are received open the packages at once, shake out the packing materials, check up the order to insure correctness, then dip the roots in water or preferably thin mud, open the bundles and trench in the garden, roots well covered with soil. This soil should be made firm to insure contact with the roots, restoring as near as possible natural conditions. If to be planted very soon, trees may be put into the cellar for a day, well watered and protected from the air.

In Planting. Your holes should be staked out and dug prior to exposing the trees. The roots by all means should be protected carefully from the sun and drying winds as either will very soon wither up the fibrous roots necessary for quick and vigorous growth. In digging the holes see that they are larger by 6 to 12 inches all around than the roots of the trees to be set in them, and deep enough to plant the trees as they formerly stood in the nursery row. A few inches of loose soil in the bottoms of the holes proves helpful to early growth of the roots. In digging deep holes, the surface soil should be kept separate from the sub-soil and in planting, use the better soil in direct contact with the root system. Take out only what trees can be planted in a reasonable time, properly protecting the roots.

Place the trees in these holes, roots spread out in their natural position, and body slightly leaning to the Southwest in exposed locations, the best soil being filled in carefully between the fibrous roots and firmly tramped. Continue filling in and treading until near the level, and see that the last few inches are applied loose, so as to retain the rainfall and moisture. Never mound up the soil, as this tends to turn the water from the trees.

Mulching the trees with manure, leaves and similar materials tends to conserve the moisture, stops the encroachment of weeds and grass, and prevents the cracking and baking of the soil, meanwhile adding fertility and insuring vigorous growth.

Wrapping the trees from the ground to the first branches with burlap or similar material, or the use of corn or tobacco stalks about the trunks of trees prevents the usual sunscald and scarring on the southwest side. Trees grown in the nursery do not get direct rays of the sun, and the bark is consequently tender.

Pruning. Some pruning is required of all trees, not moved with balls of earth attached. This is a matter of judgment, as no set or fast rules can be applied. Consider the two ideas or principles of pruning. First: To establish a balance between the tops and roots, which later have been cut and broken in digging the tree, and second: To regulate the shape of the tree and affect its growth by so pruning. The general rule is to cut in the lateral branches about half way, especially with fruit trees. With shade trees, those of fast growth should be similarly treated, while those of conical or very slow growth, may be more advantageously pruned by removing the smaller inside branches and a slight shortening of the terminals, striving to retain the natural contour of the tree.

Admonition. These suggestions are not cure-alls or guarantees of growth as Evergreens, Cherries, Nuts, Oaks, Birch, Gum, and Tulip Poplars are more difficult to make grow than others and weather conditions and care that follow do more to insure growth than expedient handling.

Apple Orchard.

# Apples

Owing to its adaptability to various soil conditions, its hardiness, productiveness, and commercial value, we must consider the apple the most important of our tree fruits. Planted only in well drained soils, with proper care taken in the selection of varieties one may expect fruit from early summer throughout the winter months. An acre or so devoted to apples, properly planted and with ordinary attention to pruning and cultivation will yield very satisfactory returns. Our list has been further reduced to only the most dependable sorts, and those listed below may be planted with confidence. As the trees develop the trimming out of the cross and crowded branches is all the pruning required. When planting apple trees permit 3 to 5 well developed branches to remain, but shorten these to 6 or 8 inches.

Varieties may become exhausted, and if so we always substitute one variety of same season and color as near as possible. There will be a shortage of good apples in the country this year.

|  | Each | 10 | 100 |
|---|---|---|---|
| Extra Size, 5-6 feet | $0.50 | $4.50 | $40.00 |
| Medium Size, 4-5 feet | .40 | 3.50 | 30.00 |

## Early Apples

**Astrachan.** Early, red, crisp and tart, excellent for cooking. Perhaps the best extra early. Reliable.

**Benoni.** Attractive, red, best eating apple of its season. Early bearer and very productive.

**Chenango Strawberry.** An August apple, striped red on yellow. Very good.

**Early Harvest.** Pale yellow, sub-acid, regular bearer and is the most popular of the old general purpose varieties.

**Early Transparent.** Very early bearer, productive, valuable for either home or market. Blights on rich soil, however. Waxy yellow, tart, excellent.

**Golden Sweet.** The Best Sweet we know. Yellow, vigorous grower, productive. Hasn't a fault. Fine.

**Liveland.** A red Transparent. Succeeds everywhere. A very promising commercial and home variety.

**Maiden's Blush.** A grand old favorite. Waxy yellow, pleasing red blush. Ripens over a long period, making it valuable for an orchard.

**Oldenburg.** Streaked yellow and red, large, crisp and tart. Best cooking and a vigorous grower. Valuable.

**Red June.** Medium sized, red, excellent quality, early bearer. Tree productive; not vigorous.

**Summer Pearmain.** Late summer, striped red on greenish-yellow. Quality the best. Old but reliable.

## Fall Apples

**Fallawater.** Greenish-yellow, extra large and sub-acid. Tree vigorous, early and regular bearer. We consider it one of the best.

**Grimes Golden.** No orchard complete without it. Yellow, best quality and productive. For either home or market for this season there is nothing better.

**Hubbardston.** Striped and dots of red on yellow. Large. We think better than Baldwin for this state.

**Northern Spy.** Large striped. Crisp, juicy, aromatic. Excellent quality. Long coming into bearing.

**Greening (N. W.)** Large pale yellowish-green. Very hardy and fine grower.

**Rambo.** An old favorite. Yellow shaded with red, medium size, tender and juicy. Supply limited.

**Wolf River.** Extra large, showy and productive. Hardy and regular.

## "Early" Winter Apples

**Baldwin.** Red, large, fine quality, tree vigorous. The commercial apple of the east.

**Delicious** Red, large and uniform in size, distinct because of five lobes on blossom end. Variety new, very popular and no orchard should be without it. Quality unexcelled. A very early and heavy bearer, good for market or home. No new apple ever had such a promising future.

**Black Twig** A seedling of Wine Sap. Larger, splashed with red, sub-acid and very productive. We can specially recommend this for Kentucky. Valuable for home or market. Try it.

**Jonathan.** An early bearing variety, red, medium size and quality very good. Tree never large but productive.

**Kinnaird.** We consider this one of the best of the Wine Sap family. Larger than old Wine Sap, darker red and productive. Does not blight.

**Milam.** A standard for 50 years. Quality excellent, color red, size medium. Well known.

**Rome Beauty** Large red, tender and sub-acid, early bearer and productive. A commercial sort in most sections, and a very popular variety.

**Stark.** An apple overlooked by many. Color greenish-red; unattractive for market, but for productiveness, regularity, vigorous growth, etc., should be in every farmer's orchard.

**Stayman Winesap** Dark, rich red, indistinctly striped; larger than old Wine Sap. Tree productive and a drought resister.

**Winesap** Medium size, dark red, productive variety, excellent quality, crisp and juicy—sub-acid. The most extensively grown, the most abundant bearer, with more good qualities in its favor than anything we have to offer for Kentucky.

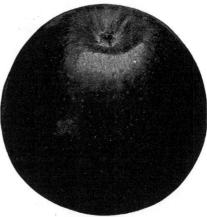

Rome Beauty.

**Wealthy.** Not fruited here yet. Large, shaded to dark red, quality good, tender and productive. Very early to bear and exceedingly promising.

**Winter Banana.** Quick maturing tree, bearing large yellowish fruit with blush. Flesh firm, flavor sub-acid and of excellent quality. A dessert apple. Very satisfactory.

## "Late" Winters

**Ben Davis.** Striped red, large and attractive. Surest bearer, healthy tree, vigorous and should be planted as a "catch" in every orchard. Only fault lacks quality.

**Gano.** Very similar to Ben Davis, better quality. Commercial sort in Middle West.

**Ingram.** Red striped, juicy and productive. Very regular bearer and is an improved Janet. New and very good.

**Janet (Rawles).** Medium sized red-greenish apple, an old favorite, being subject to rot in humid seasons.

**Romanite.** Medium sized red, quality fair. Never misses a good crop and will keep until spring. Tree vigorous and healthy.

**York Imperial** A late keeping commercial variety, shaded red on yellowish skin, flesh firm and tree healthy. Regular and heavy bearer. Plant for profit or for home.

## Crab Apples

**Hyslop.** Large, dark. Tree vigorous and productive.

**Whitney.** This is a crab really edible; late, and good for jelly or use from hand.

Delicious.

# The Peach

Light or well drained soils, preferably sandy loams seem to produce the best peaches. The tree is quick to mature, bearing heavily at an early age, and its comparative freedom from disease makes it deservedly popular. The annual pruning should consist of shortening in the terminal growth to maintain a round and compact head. When the crop is killed by severe winters as the one of 1918, "dehorning" or severe cutting in of branches is desired. The tree bears its fruit on the young wood.

The principal enemy to the tree is the "Peach Borer" that burrows under the bark below the ground line. Turning back the soil, scraping with a knife or prodding the runs with a wire is the best remedy. Boiling water poured about the trees will also kill the borer.

In planting. Prune severely. Cut away all the side branches to inch stubs and shorten back the leader to form a balanced, low and compact head.

Some varieties are limited.

|  | Each | 10 | 100 |
|---|---|---|---|
| Extra Size, 5-6 feet | $0.50 | $4.50 | $40.00 |
| Medium Size, 4-5 feet | .40 | 3.50 | 30.00 |

## Early Ripening

**Mayflower** (Free), Red all over, fine and good. The earliest peach known. June 25th. Extra hardy.

**Red Bird** (Cling). A creamy white peach almost covered with red. Large, hardy and good. An extra cling that gives promise of being a leading commercial variety. July 1-5.

**Greensboro** (Free). The very best extra early commercial sort. Hardy and productive, fruit large and tree healthy. Color, white with crimson cheek. July 1.

## Second Ripening

**Alton** (Free), White, splashed and shaded with red. Skin tough, of good quality. Hardy. About the same season as Carman but larger. July 25-August 1.

**Belle Georgia** (Free). White with decided blush, excellent quality. In Hiley and this variety we have the two best white fleshed peaches for home or market. Plant them. August 20.

**Brackett** (Free). Orange yellow mottled and blushed carmine. Large, quality the best. We have not fruited this new variety but because of its popularity we have added it to our list. About a week later than Elberta. Aug. 20-25.

Elberta.

**Carman** (Free). White with red blush. Carman is extra hardy, bears every year, and when it fails all else fails too. Tree a very robust grower and produces heavily. Next to Elberta, Carman should be considered. We are partial to it. July 20.

**Early Elberta** (Free). Well named, being a clear yellow with blush, finer grained and sweeter. Tree a strong grower, with a tendency to thin itself, carrying moderate loads of fruit. Superior to Elberta as a canning peach, and requires less sugar.

**Elberta** (Free). Beautiful yellow, large and shaded with deep red. Elberta has been the peach for years, and is just as good today. The fact is that more than 80% of commercial plantings are of this variety speaks well enough for it. August 15.

**Hiley** (Free). Cream white with decided red cheek, oblong, large, firm and of best quality. Good shipper and just a few days in advance of Georgia Belle. Hiley is a new variety and it belongs in every orchard or yard. August 1.

**Illinois** (Free). Large red and white peach with a brilliant crimson cheek. Showy. Flesh firm, juicy. Good for market or shipping. Free from rot. August 1-5.

**J. H. Hale** (Free). Yellow, almost covered with red; more highly colored than Elberta; flesh firm, melting and of best quality. Ripens August 10-15. This is the much heralded peach of J. H. Hale, the "peach king," that has been so widely advertised. We hardly have trees enough to last the whole season, but will fill in order received.

## Late Ripening

**Chair** (Free). Originated in Maryland. Fruit of very large size; deep yellow with red cheek; flesh yellow, firm and of good quality. Tree strong grower and productive. One of the best of the Crawford family. September 20.

**Heath** (Cling). White, tinged next to the sun. A large, firm, juicy peach of most pleasing flavor. Skin rather downy. Well known. October 1.

**Henrietta** (Cling). Yellow with crimson blush. A large fine fruit. Tree healthy and productive. September 20.

**Krummell** (Free). Golden yellow blushed red and carmine. Large, round, melting, subacid, good. Another new peach that is fast gaining in popularity. September 20-25.

# The Pear

The Pear thrives in a rich or deep soil. There is a wide range of varieties — the Europeans (E.) being of better quality, and the Japanese (J.) varieties more productive. The quality of the pear however, may be increased by picking before the fruit is ripe and spreading on a floor to soften. The worst enemy is pear blight, a bacterial disease that cannot be successfully controlled by spraying. On first appearance of the terminals withering, prune them out below the injured part and burn. Winter spraying with suitable fungicides will help. Do not encourage too vigorous growth. At planting time prune as you do the apple.

|  | Each | 10 | 100 |
|---|---|---|---|
| Extra Size, 5-6 feet | $0.65 | $6.00 | $55.00 |
| Medium Size, 4-5 feet | .55 | 5.00 | 45.00 |

**Anjou.** (E). Fine large; flesh fine grained and vinous. Tree is hardy and productive.

**Bartlett** (E). The best known and most popular of all. An early, abundant bearer, of superior quality. Large, with a beautiful blush next the sun. Delicious for eating.

**Clapp's Favorite.** (E). A seedling of Bartlett, but larger, earlier and as valuable. Tree vigorous and productive, upright grower.

**Duchess.** (E). A large, rich, buttery pear, and does well on most soils.

**Early Harvest.** (E). Large, yellow, with cheek of red; very early; fair quality; not disposed to blight. Tree vigorous grower.

**Howell.** (E). Large, yellow; of fine quality; ripening September 1; an early and abundant bearer.

**Kieffer** (J). Large golden yellow when ripened, sometimes red blotched on sun-exposed side. Flesh very firm, crisp and juicy, especially prized for canning. To properly ripen gather carefully and place in a dark warm place of even temperature. Tree is vigorous, early bearer and free from disease. Commercial variety.

**Lawrence.** (E). Most valuable of winter pears; medium size; flesh melting and rich. Tree is hardy, productive, and an early bearer.

**Seckel.** (E). A well-known, small, russety fruit; the most exquisite of pears; of slow growth in nursery row. September.

Kieffer Pear.

# The Plum

Demands good soil, and can be used as a filler in the orchard between permanent trees, in back yards, gardens and especially in the chicken runs. Thinning of the fruit is advised in wet seasons or when trees are overloaded.

The European varieties (E.) are of better quality, the American or native (A.) varieties for hardiness and the Japans (J.) for early bearing.

Some varieties in limited supply.

|  | Each | 10 | 100 |
|---|---|---|---|
| Extra Size, 5-6 feet | $0.65 | $6.00 | $55.00 |
| Medium Size, 4-5 feet | .55 | 5.00 | 45.00 |

**Abundance.** (J). The hardiest and most prolific of the Japans. Large, oval, amber changing to bright cherry.

**Burbank.** (J). Variety of large size; violet with yellow flesh. Very hardy and productive. Follows later than Abundance.

**Damson.** (E). Too well known to describe. Succeeds everywhere.

**Endicott.** A hybrid. Color, amber; tree vigorous and productive, good quality.

**Green Gage.** (E). Medium size; yellow with plume; flesh soft, rich, and aromatic; very popular.

**Imperial Gage.** (E). Very similar to above and larger. Later than Green Gage.

**Lombard.** (E). Large; color, bright purple. Great market variety being prolific.

**Milton.** (A). Ripens in July; large; bright red; quality better than the old standard Wild Goose.

**Omaha.** American-Japanese hybrid. Pleasing coral red with yellow flesh. Productive and of best quality.

**Red June.** (J). An early red variety, prolific and popular.

**Wild Goose.** (A). Size medium; color, deep red; quality good. Bears every year and most dependable of the plums. Very valuable.

**Yellow Japan.** (J). Large early plum of a pleasing yellow color. Quality good, and tree heavy bearer.

Burbank Plums.

# The Cherry

Cherries succeed only in the drier soils, preferring types that are porous or stony to the low and heavier lands required by other tree fruits. The sours and sub-acid group are more productive of fruit, quick to bear and dependable. The sweet or Hearts are vigorous of tree but not constant producers. Pruning the bearing trees is seldom necessary, save sawing broken or mutilated branches.

At planting time, shorten in the branches about half way and tread the earth very firmly about the roots. Cherry trees can be planted close to the house, and the value of the fruit is not surpassed by any other on the market.

Some varieties in limited supply.

|  | Each | 10 | 100 |
|---|---|---|---|
| Extra Size, 5-6 feet | $0.65 | $6.00 | $55.00 |
| Medium Size, 4-5 feet | .55 | 5.00 | 45.00 |

## Dukes

**Early Richmond.** The standard tart cherry that yields nearly every year and reddens the tree with the abundance of its yield, succeeding everywhere.

**Late Duke.** This is almost like the succeeding, only it ripens more uniformly.

**May Duke.** A compact, vigorous tree; fruit large, red, and when fully ripe mildly sub-acid. One of the best.

**Montmorency.** This variety is supplanting Early Richmond as a commercial sort, because of its larger size and productiveness. Ripens a week later than Early Richmond.

## Hearts and Biggareaus

**Black Tartarian.** Best known and most valuable of Heart cherries; fruit large, dark, half-tender, rich and pleasant. Tree hardy, vigorous and productive.

Black Tartarian.

**Gov. Wood.** Pale with blush, fruit medium, flesh soft, and best known of table cherries.

**Napoleon.** Almost identical in fruit with Yellow Spanish, but tree more erect. A prince among its kind.

**Rockport.** A grand mid-season cherry that is unequaled for use from hand.

**Windsor.** This is a modern Black Tartarian and holds second place to none, and is generally known as Ox Heart.

**Yellow Spanish.** A grand, firm, late, yellow fruit that in one form or another is admired all around the world.

## Compass Cherry

A cross between a plum and cherry, the fruit resembling the former and the tree the latter. This hybrid is especially valuable for its hardiness and early bearing, often fruiting in the nursery row. About the size and shape of a Damson, but red. Quality fair to good. We have only a limited supply and offer at same price as plum trees as long as they last.

|  | Each | 10 |
|---|---|---|
| Extra Size, 4-5 foot trees | $0.65 | $6.00 |
| Medium Size, 3½-4 foot trees | .55 | 5.00 |

# Quince

Luxuriates in good, deep ground, and on such will quickly yield an abundance of fruit just the best to preserve or for jelly. We have tried all the standard kinds, but the Orange has done by far the best with us.

|  | Each | 10 |
|---|---|---|
| 3-4 feet | $0.50 | $4.50 |
| 2-3 feet | .45 | 4.00 |

# Persimmons

The persimmon is the last of the fruits to ripen, hanging on the tree until well into the winter. It requires care in planting and sharp pruning. It bears in a few years and is long lived. This native fruit often forms a pleasant link in the sweet chain of memories of the old home.

|  | Each | 10 |
|---|---|---|
| 4-5 feet | $0.75 | $6.00 |

# The Grape

This ancient fruit is at home on any character of soil and there is not a place that should be without them. Whether in the vineyards or arbors, back yards, or trained on fences, porches or buildings, the grape bears with astonishing regularity. The secret of successful growing lies in proper pruning. The annual growth should be cut back to 3 or 4 buds each season, removing entirely the weak canes. As the vines produce better on the younger wood, constant renewing from the bottom by encouraging new shoots every few years is recommended.

At planting time shorten the roots to 14-16 inches, and the tops to two or three joints and lay in trenches eight inches deep, with only the buds showing. By placing the roots all in one direction, stakes or posts may be renewed at any time without damage to the roots. Prune back the first season's growth, and the second summer train but two vigorous canes to stakes. At the end of the growing season shorten these to 4-6 feet depending on the vigor of the plant, training off laterals to cover your wires or buildings from these. Some varieties very scarce.

|                                        | Each   | 10     | 100     |
|----------------------------------------|--------|--------|---------|
| 2 Year, No. 1 Vines                    | $0.35  | $3.00  | $25.00  |

By parcel post add 25 cents for 10 vines.

## Black Grapes

**Campbell Early.** A well-known, new grape that really has with us, failed to live up to its good reputation. An extra early sort.

**Concord.** This is without doubt the best general purpose grape grown. Its planting perhaps equals that of all the other varieties combined. Berry large. Bunches shouldered and fairly compact.

**Cottage.** A seedling of the above. Ten days earlier; not quite as good quality, but desirable for its season.

**Ives.** For hardiness and productiveness this grape has no equal. Quality not equal to Concord, but ripens earlier and will hang on the vine until shriveled. To mix with Concord for wine or grape juice this is unsurpassed.

**Isabella.** A late, large, black grape, with a delightful musky flavor. Bunches loose.

**Worden.** A seedling of Concord, of better quality. Ripens ten days earlier. Bunch and berry large, compact. Not quite so hardy or long-lived, however, it should be planted in every collection.

## Red Grapes

**Agawam.** Bunches medium and irregular; berries large; exceedingly delightful, meaty grape. Valuable for home use.

**Brighton.** Large, compact, shouldered bunch, with medium to large berry; juicy, sweet, good. Unsurpassed for table.

**Catawba.** The standard late red grape that has lost none of its popularity. Its season and quality make it indispensable.

**Delaware.** The best known red grape. Bunch and berry small, compact. Flavor unsurpassed. Not a strong grower; must be given good, rich soil.

**Moyer.** Resembling Delaware very much in color, size and quality and a more vigorous grower.

**Lindley.** Of exceptionally good quality, large, ripening in mid-season. Vigorous of vine and hardy.

**Lucille.** A new grape of decided merit. Very hardy, likely to overbear if not pruned severely. Bunch very compact, color light red.

**Lutie.** An early grape of good size. Its  p  p        makes the vine scarce.

**Salem.** A late grape of decided merit. Berry large and juicy, pleasing flavor and because of its season, very valuable.

**Wyoming.** Bunch and berry small but perfect. A hardy, productive variety of excellent quality. We grow more of this than any other red grape.

## White Grapes

**Martha.** An old standard white grape of merit.

**Niagara.** The best white grape; bunch and berry large, meaty and juicy. Flavor perfect. Well known.

**Pocklington.** Another seedling of Concord, of about the same size. Quality good.

Concord Grapes.

# Raspberries

Loose soils produce the best raspberries. Partial shade is no hindrance to productiveness, as the natural habitat of the raspberries is in lower ground, filled with leaf mold and partly shaded. For this reason along higher fences and in between the young orchard trees, raspberries are found to thrive. Allow not more than five good canes to develop to the plant, and pinch out the tops of these when they attain a height of 3-4 feet in order to encourage laterals. After the fruit has been picked, cut out all the old canes to allow plenty of room for the new ones to develop. Plant 3x5 feet apart and prune off all tops that show more than 2 inches above the ground.

Both the pink and black raspberries are sold only in bundles of 25 plants. Less than this number is hardly worth the trial.

By parcel post, 20c per 50 additional.

| Per 25 | 100 | 1,000 |
|--------|------|--------|
| $0.50 | $2.00 | $17.50 |

## Red Raspberries

**Cuthbert.** Crimson, large, conical, firm and juicy. The canes are upright, strong and vigorous. Hardy. The standard late red market and home variety that is popular and unsurpassed.

**Miller Red.** Bright scarlet, sweet and melting. This early red is the best of its season because of hardiness, productiveness and general good qualities. Ripens two weeks before Cuthbert.

**St. Regis.** The so-called everbearer. It does produce some berries throughout the summer, and in the spring is an excellent producer. Quality very good.

Cumberland Raspberries.

## Blackcap Raspberries

By parcel post, 20c per 50 additional.

| Per 25 | 100 | 1,000 |
|--------|------|--------|
| $0.75 | $3.00 | $25.00 |

**Cumberland.** Large, glossy, black, rather oval. Firm and stands handling well. After fruiting eight or ten new kinds this season we have come to the conclusion that no black raspberry of its season compares with it.

**Kansas.** The great market variety, more generally planted than any other kind; early, large, productive, round, firm, moderately juicy, a strong grower. Handsome appearance; stands shipping well.

# Blackberries

In a state where wild blackberries are so plentiful one without experience would hesitate to plant blackberries. However, the cultivated varieties are so prolific, so easy of culture, that every garden should contain this fruit. The soil to be ideal should be a heavy type—clay loam. This so-called "poor man's fruit" if planted 7x3 feet will each year, more than pay for the space it occupies. Many plant too close for best results Topping in the young shoots just as they reach 3½-4½ feet to develop the side branches to fruiting condition is the only pruning required, save the removing of the old canes after they have produced a crop.

| Per 25 | 100 | 1,000 |
|--------|------|--------|
| $0.75 | $3.00 | $25.00 |

By parcel post, 20c per 50 additional.

**Early Harvest.** Extra earliness and productiveness make this the leading commercial and home variety. Is through with its crop when the wild ones begin to ripen. Hangs well onto the canes and is a money maker.

**Eldorado.** A large, oblong, conical berry, with small seed and core; sweet and juicy; hardy and productive.

Early Harvest Blackberries.

# Currants

Thrive in deep soils, and when properly manured and cultivated will yield bountiful returns. The insect enemy causing the most injury to the currant and gooseberry alike is a leaf worm that can be killed by spraying the foliage with arsenate of lead or paris green as you do potatoes for the beetle. These return at intervals of a few years and not necessarily prevalent every season. The pruning of the older plants consists in leaving a fair amount of the three and four year wood, as it is more productive of fruit. In planting, allow about 4 feet each way for development and prune in most of the top immediately after setting.

2-year heavy plants only.

| Each | 10 | 100 |
|------|------|------|
| $0.20 | $1.50 | $10.00 |

Add 20 cents per 10 for postage.

**Red Dutch.** By far the most productive of the many kinds we have tested. Color of fruit a brilliant red, large berries borne in long clusters along the stems and quality excellent. The white varieties have proven worthless in this climate.

## Gooseberries

Very productive and are always in demand. When allowed to ripen they lose much of the sourness attributed to them because they are usually offered to the public while green. Note pruning and cultural directions for currants. Plant 4x4 feet, getting the earth well worked into the roots and firm. Prune off the tops to a few inches in order to insure growth.

2-year plants only.

| Each | 10 | 100 |
|------|------|------|
| $0.20 | $1.50 | $10.00 |

Add 20 cents per 10 for postage.

**Downing.** Fruit almost round, large, and juicy. Best quality. Whitish green color. Does especially well in the North.

**Houghton.** Round, dark red when ripe; juicy, sweet. Thin, smooth skin. Medium size. The bush is hardy, very productive, free from mildew, and the best for general purpose in this section.

## Strawberries

We make the growing of strawberry plants a specialty and as they are planted in the spring only, we issue at that time an annual catalog, devoted principally to the description of varieties and complete cultural directions. The shallow root of the strawberry does not permit planting in the fall, as the alternate freezing and thawing or expansion and settling of the surface soils throughout our falls, winters and early springs will expose the roots and cause the loss of the plants. We expect to have our usual supply, something over a million plants of best adapted varieties, as our blocks at this time give much promise.

Red Dutch Currants.

## Nut Trees

Nut trees are a looming possibility, the joy of children and the pride of their owner. As a class they do not transplant kindly in large sizes, nor grow quickly, but they grow vigorously when established and are noble trees. Many farms contain land that would be far better planted to nut trees than anything else, and would pay better than farm crops, besides annually growing more valuable as timber. We offer fine stocks of nut trees.

| | Each | 10 |
|------|------|------|
| Extra Size | $0.75 | $6.00 |

**Almond** (Hardshell). This popular nut from the South is known to everyone. The hardshell variety, though not as sweet, bears abundantly when its early blossoms are not killed by the frost. Resembles a peach in form and foliage.

**Chestnut** (American). Too well known to need comment, further than that in either form, fruit, flower or foliage—it is unsurpassed.

**Hazelnut.** Well known; productive. The plants offered are from the best English nuts.

**Pecan.** A noble native tree that yields a nut only second to English walnut in popularity.

Seedling varieties, 60 cts. each.

**Budded Pecans.** These are named sorts, doing well in the South, bearing early, nuts of better quality and size. These "paper-shell" varieties at $1.50 each.

**Walnut** (White or Butternut). Most satisfactory of the nut trees. Transplants easily, grows and bears early and abundantly.

# Asparagus

Asparagus is the earliest and best of all esculents and the easiest to grow if many old ideas be discarded. It is one of the most persistent of plants—tough as dock, but even dock can be killed over the same lines that cause people to fail with asparagus. There are two ways to grow asparagus. The owner of a town lot needs a bed five feet wide and as long as he wishes. Let it be made cream rich, spaded over, and three rows eighteen inches apart be drawn through it with a six-inch hoe, and say, four inches deep. Then the crowns should be spread out in these just as near like a spider as possible. Then let the earth be raked over and let this bed be kept clean and free of weeds for all time and well manured.

The gardener, with a plow and ample ground, can do better. Let him lay off rows five or six feet wide, and plant and manage just as indicated. After two years' growth, the town man must fork over his bed, but the farmer can just cut the earth from the rows and turn it back. The old idea was to set the roots a foot deep, so that the shoots might be long and white. The new idea is to let the plant grow like any other and then mound over the crown when the shoots are wanted otherwise than nature intended, and at the end of that time to plow the earth and restore normal conditions. This can be done by the large grower, but the town man can only heap more manure and force the plant to make a new tier of roots nearer the surface. Asparagus wants to be near the surface like any other plant, and if we will heap the earth over them for a long time and then remove it when shoots long, white and tender are no longer needed, grandchildren will bless the hand that planted. The things that cause failure are planting near trees or vines, the covering of plants so deep that resurrection is impossible, the mowing of tops while green, the covering with salt and the rioting of weeds. Moles do not injure; no pit is needed nor wall of stone, but only the practice suggested. There are thousands of beds ruined by some of these malpractices, for which nothing can be done except to plant a new bed and treat the old in the meantime with ordinary plant prudence. The plants may be set with equal certainty either fall or spring.

The rust, so destructive for some years on asparagus generally, has disappeared, and the plants are now perfectly healthy. We have never grown so large and fine a stock and can furnish all orders—great or small.

2-year plants, per 50, $1.00; per 100, $2.00.

Parcel post, 10c per 100; 25c per 50 additional.

## Rhubarb

Rhubarb or pie plant is known to everyone. Planted 4x3 with eye 4 inches below the surface on cream rich soil, success is assured. We offer only divided crowns and not seedling plants as these are worthless.

| Each | 10 | 100 |
|---|---|---|
| $0.10 | $1.00 | $8.00 |

By parcel post, 15c per 10 additional.

**Excelsior.** Very early with long stem. Plant vigorous and dependable.

**Victoria.** Later than above, heavier of stalk and of good quality.

Asparagus.

## Sage

Each, 10c; 10, 50c.

By parcel post, add 15c per 10.

A well known plant for the garden, of easy culture and long lived. The leaves are indispensable for certain seasonings.

## Horseradish

Per 10, 25c; 100 for $2.00.

By parcel post, add 10c per 10.

The roots serve as an excellent relish. Once established is of very easy culture.

## Seed Potatoes

Second Crop Seed Potatoes, or those planted in July and matured in late fall assure seed of the best quality. We have been growers for years and we know that our seed potatoes matured weeks after the "Northern Seed," owing to the nature of the potato, will give much better returns. We have selected for several years only smooth potatoes, true to type, and therefore offer seed of insured quality. Descriptions and prices will be included in our spring catalog.

# Ornamental Department

The home grounds should be made as attractive as the home itself. To the interior of our homes we add decorations, pictures, draperies, furnishings and fixtures, designed with an idea of comfort, beauty and convenience; but if we leave untouched and unplanted the home grounds we have failed greatly to realize the real beauties of a home or to understand the real significance of the word.

We offer a wide assortment of such ornamental and fruit stock designed to meet the requirements of our patrons. Many of our trees are native—and therefore we know they will thrive better than many imported and unadapted species. In blooming shrubs, the list is long, the color range is wide and those especially adapted to certain locations are described. In Evergreens, we can furnish for lawn or foundation, specimens for either purpose.

Landscaping. For those who cannot avail themselves of a good landscape architect we offer these suggestions.

In placing the drives and walks, remember that graceful curves are more pleasing than straight lines, avoiding when possible terraces and steep banks by proper grading as care taking and upkeep will be less. In planting strive to preserve the desirable views, screening the objectionable. Nothing is more pleasing than an open and well kept lawn, so attempt to leave as much open space as possible, planting along the borders and roadways with groups of shrubs and trees arranged in irregular bays or projections. In grouping your plants attempt to get the finer and smaller varieties in the foreground, planting those of bolder outline in the distance to add character. Use those plants suitable for your soil and conditions, arranging the hardy or long-lived varieties for permanency, and the rapid maturing varieties for immediate effect, to be later cut out. Such simple suggestions are suitable to the large and small estate.

Fraxinus Americana—American White Ash.

## Free Booklet

We distribute a 48-page booklet—"Home Grounds —Their Planning and Planting," edited by a practical landscape architect, covering the arrangement of trees and shrubs for the lawn and house and similar planting that may be undertaken about the home. Those intending to do any considerable planting would do well to get a copy of this, being free on request from any patron. This booklet deals concisely with every idea, including numerous illustrations, and ground plans of lawns, suggestions for foundation plantings, drives and walks, perennial borders, vegetable garden, etc.

# Deciduous Trees

There is an ornamental deciduous tree for almost every purpose—whether for shade, for hiding objectionable sights, for beauty of flower, or utility. Knowing them as we do, there is not one but has its faults, and therefore careful choosing of your trees should follow. We commend the use of shade trees not only as specimens but in groups thickly planted and bordered with shrubs. We carry a very complete line of adaptable shade trees, properly grown with heavy roots to insure vigor.

We call your attention to the planting suggestions offered on page 2, in this catalog for your use. Also on this page mention has been made of trees best suited for special purposes. Trees bring a natural beauty to a place whether a lawn or a pasture lot, street, avenue or park. We exhort everyone to plant trees of this character, for their beauty and comfort. Plant large, growing trees 40 feet apart, and those not so robust at 30. For immediate effect planting at 20 feet, with an idea of later removing each alternate one, is commended to those desiring shade at once.

At planting time prune as suggested on page 2. Pruning is a matter of judgment, and if properly done, at the same time getting the earth well worked and tramped into the root system trees should live in satisfactory proportions.

It is difficult to say in each description just what trees and plants are available for various purposes and therefore follows a list of trees better adapted to these special purposes. While everything we list is suitable on the lawn for shade or scenic effect this list will give the patron a quick reference list.

### AVENUE TREES.

| | |
|---|---|
| Ash | Norway Maple |
| Elm | Sugar Maple |
| Gum | Sycamore |
| European Linden | Pin Oak |
| Silver Maple | Lombardy Poplar |

### TREES THAT COLOR IN THE FALL

| | |
|---|---|
| Ash | Oak |
| Dogwood | Tulip Poplar |
| Sweet Gum | Varnish, Japan |
| Maples | Sumac |

### TREES FOR QUICK EFFECT

| | |
|---|---|
| Ash | Paulownia |
| Catalpa | Lombardy Poplar |
| Silver Maple | Sycamore |
| Russian Mulberry | Weeping Willow |

### TREES THAT FLOWER

| | |
|---|---|
| Catalpa | Magnolia |
| Dogwood, White | Paulownia |
| Dogwood, Red | Tulip Poplar |
| Horse Chestnut | Red Bud |
| Linden | Crab Apple |

### ODD AND CONSPICUOUS

| | |
|---|---|
| Purple Beech | Magnolia |
| Weeping Birch | Weeping Mulberry |
| Catalpa Bungei | Japan Varnish |
| Cypress | Schwedleri Maple |
| Kentucky Coffee | Red Bud |
| Larch | Weeping Willow |
| Maiden Hair | |

## Ash - Fraxinus

Native trees of quick growth, thriving on dry or moist soils. Branches spreading, foliage healthy, growth rapid and easy to transplant should make them even more popular than they are.

**American Ash** (F. Americana). A stately native tree, with straight clean growth; foliage light green. Dependable and very satisfactory as it grows rapidly, being a forest tree valuable for timber.

**Green Ash** (F. viridis). There is a slight difference between these varieties. The young wood is inclined to be square, hence the botanical name. The foliage in the fall is a light green, changing to a rose tint before the leaves fall. The leaves are roundish and rather large for the species. Very quick to take hold when transplanted.

**European Ash** (F. Excelsior). This tree is not often planted as persons are not familiar with its good qualities. It is very rapid, spreading in habit of growth. The leaves are very dark green, narrow and pointed but nevertheless is very fine for shade. The bark is gray and the buds on the young wood are black. For specimen, group or natural plantings this tree is recommended.

| | Each | 10 |
|---|---|---|
| 6- 8 feet | $0.75 | $7.00 |
| 8-10 feet | 1.00 | 9.00 |
| 10-12 feet | 1.50 | 12.50 |
| 12-14 feet | 2.00 | 17.50 |

## Beech - Fagus

The beeches are most attractive. When properly grown, with their low spreading branches and general symmetry of growth they are one of the most popular trees for lawn use. The leaves remain late in the year and for that reason for screening purposes are frequently planted. While not very rapid in growth, the effect produced is worthy of the wait. Firm soil well about the roots.

**European Beech** (F. Sylvatica). The foliage is a silvery green, the young growth and under sides of the leaves being especially noticeable. Like the native varieties holds the foliage well and colors vividly in the fall.

| | Each | 10 |
|---|---|---|
| 7- 9 feet | $1.50 | $12.50 |
| 6- 8 feet | 1.25 | 10.00 |
| 5- 6 feet | 1.00 | 9.00 |

**Purple or Copper Beech** (F. Purpurea). Thus called because of its especially dark purple foliage. In the spring, when first in leaf the richness of its color must be seen to be appreciated. In midsummer it holds its color well but changes to a crimson in the fall. For brightening dull shades in shrub borders, planted as specimens on the lawn or in the foreground of light colored buildings for contrast it can be highly recommended.

| | Each | 10 |
|---|---|---|
| 7-9 feet | $2.00 | $17.50 |
| 6-8 feet | 1.75 | 15.00 |
| 5-6 feet | 1.50 | 12.50 |

White Flowering Dogwood—Cornus Florida.

## Birch - Betula

Conspicuous trees with their white bark, clean growth, small and pendant young wood. Native to moist places but nevertheless when transplanted on dry ground seem to thrive equally as well. Planted as specimen trees, in borders for screen effect or grouped against buildings or better in contrast with evergreens, the winter effect is wonderful.

White Birch (B. alba). Tree of quick vigorous growth, bark is almost white, erect growing with terminal branches slightly drooping. A very satisfactory tree that should be more widely used.

| | Each | 10 |
|---|---|---|
| 8-10 feet | $1.50 | $12.50 |
| 7- 9 feet | 1.25 | 10.00 |
| 6- 8 feet | 1.00 | 9.00 |

Weeping White Birch (B. alba pendula). This tree is one of the most conspicuous trees grown. With its white bark, deeply cut leaves and long pendant branches it presents a picturesque effect planted either as a specimen or otherwise. It should be pruned well when planted and once established will prove of great merit.

| | Each | 10 |
|---|---|---|
| 7-9 feet | $1.75 | $15.00 |
| 6-8 feet | 1.25 | 10.00 |

Purple Birch (B. purpurea). Tree is a typical birch, bark a dark color and the leaves purple in color. Branches follow the general birch habit—and drooping gracefully.

| | Each | 10 |
|---|---|---|
| 6-8 feet | $1.25 | $10.00 |

## Catalpa

Umbrella Catalpa (C. Bungei). This tree has become popular because of its straight stems and symmetrical roundish heads which resemble an umbrella. The tops are dwarf and while they do not grow very rapidly their wide leaves give them the appearance of much larger trees. The foliage is very pleasing and the effect obtained when planted in pairs along walks, drives or entrances is greatly admired.

| | Each | 10 |
|---|---|---|
| 2-year heads, 5-6 feet | $1.50 | $12.50 |

Western Catalpa (C. Speciosa). This is a tree of very quick growth, and thousands of seedling trees have been planted for timber. The growth is astonishing when planted on moist land, but thrives on higher and poorer soil. The tree in June is a mass of white bloom and therefore highly desirable when flower effect is desired. The catalpas sometimes suffer from blight—the branches wilt and die, but the tree is never killed.

| | Each | 10 |
|---|---|---|
| 8-10 feet | $1.00 | $9.00 |
| 7-9 feet | .75 | 6.00 |

## Cypress - Taxodium

Bald Cypress (T. distichum). This is very conspicuous with its pyramidal growth. unusual bark, fine, feathery, light green foliage—a cone bearing tree but unusual because it is deciduous. Native to moist soils but some of the best specimens seen are on soils entirely free of drainage water. To persons desiring something unusual in trees the Cypress is recommended.

| | Each | 10 |
|---|---|---|
| 7-9 feet | $1.50 | $12.50 |
| 6-8 feet | 1.25 | 10.00 |
| 5-6 feet | 1.00 | 9.00 |

## Dogwood - Cornus

White Flowering Dogwood (C. Florida). A native tree known to everyone. Of irregular shape but very desirable for flower effect in the early spring before its leaves appear. In the fall colors wonderfully before shedding. Planted in groups, as a background for a shrub border or planted in contrast with the flowering Red Bud proves a small tree worthy of extensive planting.

| | Each | 10 |
|---|---|---|
| 4-5 feet | $0.75 | $6.00 |
| 3-4 feet | .60 | .5.00 |
| 2-3 feet | .50 | 4.00 |

Red or Pink Flowering Dogwood (C. Florida rubra). This is a colored form of the above native sort, resembling it very closely in habit of growth, period of bloom and general behavior. Conspicuous in the early spring with its bright bloom of deep rose color.

| | Each | 10 |
|---|---|---|
| 3-4 feet | $1.50 | $12.50 |

## Elm - Ulmus

American Elm (U. Americana). A tree of unusual vigor, a native too well known to describe. It is rapid of growth, with its long spreading and pendant branches forming giant arches over roads and streets or as a lawn tree is quick to make a marked effect. The wood is tough, the leaves are moderate in size and makes a permanent tree for shade. The beetle that defoliates the European elms avoids these.

Slippery or Red Elm (U. fulva). A tree of very rapid growth, more so than above named variety. The branches are long and clean of bark, the leaves larger. The bark is used for medicinal purposes and perhaps this makes the tree especially well known.

Large specimens specially priced in Elms.

| | Each | 10 |
|---|---|---|
| 12-14 feet | $2.50 | $22.50 |
| 10-12 feet | 2.00 | 17.50 |
| 8-10 feet | 1.50 | 12.50 |
| 7- 9 feet | 1.00 | 9.00 |

## Gum - Liquidambar

Sweet Gum (L. Styraciflua). Another native tree not appreciated. It is not of rapid growth nor especially easy to transplant, but the glossy foliage in summer, the brilliant color in the fall and the unusual appearance in the winter of the young branches with their corky bark are considerations that make it especially valuable. Should be planted more generally.

| | Each | 10 |
|---|---|---|
| 10-12 feet | $2.50 | $20.00 |
| 8-10 feet | 1.50 | 12.50 |
| 7- 9 feet | 1.25 | 10.00 |
| 6- 8 feet | 1.00 | 9.00 |

## Hackberry - Celtis

Hackberry or Nettle Tree (C. occidentalis). A tree resembling the Elm somewhat but of more erect growth. Used sometimes as a street tree. The fruit is attractive to birds and small boys in fall and early winter.

| | Each | 10 |
|---|---|---|
| 7-9 feet | $1.50 | $12.50 |
| 6-8 feet | 1.25 | 10.00 |

## Horse Chestnut - Aesculus

European Horse Chestnut (A. hippocastanum). A tree of slow growth, yet very attractive in its roundish form with large leaves that are conspicuous in early summer. There is a leaf rust that affects the foliage late in the summer that detracts somewhat from the good qualities of the tree. It is specially valued for the long panicles of flowers, white and tinged with red.

| | Each | 10 |
|---|---|---|
| 7-9 feet | $1.50 | $12.50 |
| 6-8 feet | 1.25 | 10.00 |

## Varnish Tree - Koelreuteria

Japanese Varnish Tree (K. Paniculata). A tree unusual in form and character, being irregular in wood growth, but forming a roundish head of bright green foliage. The terminals of the branches are surmounted in July with showy yellow flowers in large panicles. The foliage in fall changes to a bright but pleasing yellow. Valued for unusual or odd places or in the background of the shrub border.

| | Each | 10 |
|---|---|---|
| 4-5 feet | $0.75 | $6.00 |

## Kentucky Coffee - Gymnocladus

Kentucky Coffee (G. canadensis). Native to Kentucky. Very blunt sturdy branches, inconspicuous buds developing into frond-shaped leaves, giving the tree a more tropical appearance than any other native. Flowers inconspicuous but superbly fragrant.

| | Each | 10 |
|---|---|---|
| 7-9 feet | $1.25 | $10.00 |
| 5-6 feet | 1.00 | 9.00 |

## Larch - Larix

European Larch (L. Europa). Like the cypress. A deciduous tree bearing cones like evergreens. The foliage is very fine, needle-like, appearing earlier in the spring than any other tree and stays until very late fall. The tree is a perfect pyramid in shape, hold its contour until maturity. Very conspicuous because of bright green color, unusual needles, and branching habit. We recommend it for city planting also, as the foliage does not seem to be affected by smoke and dust.

| | Each | 10 |
|---|---|---|
| 8-10 feet | $1.50 | $12.50 |
| 7- 9 feet | 1.25 | 10.00 |
| 6- 8 feet | 1.00 | 9.00 |

European Linden—Tilia Europea.

## Liriodendron - Tulip Tree

Tulip Tree or Tulip Poplar (L. Tulipifera). So called because of the resemblance of the blossoms to the tulip. It is a native of forest growth, known as Yellow Poplar and valued therefore for its wood. It is botanically classified as a magnolia and in May when its large leathery leaves have formed, it comes in full blossom, of creamy yellow, making a beautiful sight. Should be transplanted in small sizes, as it does not move as kindly as some trees. Its cleanly habit, quick growth after established a year or so and when given deep or moist soil thrives with unusual vigor.

| | Each | 10 |
|---|---|---|
| 8-10 feet | $1.50 | $12.50 |
| 7-9 feet | 1.25 | 10.00 |
| 6-8 feet | 1.00 | 9.00 |

## Linden - Basswood - Tilia

European Linden (Tilia Europea). A very compact, pyramidal tree, of dark green foliage, easy to transplant and very satisfactory for avenue or lawn planting. The leaves are large, heart-shaped, the branches are smooth and tough and when the tree blooms, which it does profusely, the fragrance is noticeable for considerable distance.

Broad Leaved European Linden (Tilia platyphyllos). About the same as above save the tree is inclined to be taller, the leaves larger and of a lighter green.

| | Each | 10 |
|---|---|---|
| 8-10 feet | $1.50 | $12.50 |
| 7- 9 feet | 1.25 | 10.00 |
| 6- 8 feet | 1.00 | 9.00 |

## Magnolia

Cucumber Tree (M. acuminata). A native well known in our mountains, growing conical in shape, having large, glaucous green leaves, making it very attractive. The flowers are fragrant, usually of dull white color followed by elongated green seed clusters which later turn into coral in color. Very satisfactory.

| | Each | 10 |
|---|---|---|
| 7-9 feet | $1.50 | $12.50 |
| 6-8 feet | 1.25 | 10.00 |
| 4-5 feet | 1.00 | 9.00 |

## Maiden Hair - Ginkgo or Salisburia

**Maiden Hair Tree** (Ginkgo biloba). A con-
ifer but deciduous. It is allied to the pine
family. On close examination of the leaves
one will note the aborted pine needles bound
together into a solid leaf. It is of Asiatic
origin and carries with it the indescribable
oriental appearance in the shape and position
of its branches, leaves, character of growth
and color of bark. Perfectly hardy here and in
the East largely used for avenue trees.

|  | Each | 10 |
|---|---|---|
| 8-10 feet | $1.50 | $12.50 |
| 7- 9 feet | 1.25 | 10.00 |
| 6- 8 feet | 1.00 | 9.00 |

## The Maples - Acer

As a group they contain the most popular
trees that are planted today, and justly so.
For quick effect, shade, brilliancy of color
adaptability to all conditions there is nothing
to compare with the maple family. We have
several varieties in variable sizes, all very good
when used in their proper places.

**Silver or Water Maple** (A. dasycarpum). Because of its quick growth, good foliage and
ease to transplant this tree is in great demand.
The tree blooms very early in the spring, leaves
appear promptly, being light green in color but
silvery beneath, and these remain until late
fall. For planting as temporary trees—that is,
alternating between the hard wooded and slower growers, or Oaks, Elms, Sugar Maples, Gum,
etc., this variety is highly recommended. We
grow large blocks of these and can fill your
order with large or small trees in quantities.

|  | Each | 10 |
|---|---|---|
| 16-18 feet | $5.00 | $45.00 |
| 10-12 feet | 1.50 | 12.50 |
| 8-10 feet | 1.00 | 9.00 |
| 6- 8 feet | .75 | 6.00 |

**Sugar Maple** (A. saccharinum). Known everywhere and is so popular that it is difficult to
keep a well grown supply on hand. Tree
grows to be of great size, foliage of good color
and in the fall turns indescribably to all tints
imaginable. Being of erect, conical growth,
perfectly hardy and wood of such texture that
it will survive any abnormal condition of the
weather and its adaptability to all types of
soils make it a variety justly popular. Native
grown it proves valuable for the timber for
hard wood finishing and also "tapped" for
maple sugar.

|  | Each | 10 |
|---|---|---|
| 12-14 feet | $2.50 | $20.00 |
| 10-12 feet | 2.00 | 17.50 |
| 8-10 feet | 1.50 | 12.50 |
| 6- 8 feet | 1.00 | 9.00 |

**Sycamore Maple** (A. Pseudoplatanus). A
tree resembling in growth the Norway Maple,
having deep green and decidedly ribbed leaves,
round and spreading in habit and a rapid
grower.

|  | Each | 10 |
|---|---|---|
| 8-10 feet | $1.50 | $12.50 |
| 7- 9 feet | 1.25 | 10.00 |

**Norway Maple** (A. platanoides). A tree resembling the preceding character, but of darker and large foliage, round and spreading in
habit of growth. It is really the European
hard maple and retains this character here.
For lawn, as specimens or shade, to plant on
streets beneath wires or for spreading over
sidewalks, parks, cemeteries or for avenues or
arching for roadways this tree is highly recommended. Sometimes the trunks are inclined to

*Silver Maple—Acer dasycarpum.*

be slightly crooked when young, but it is well
known they grow out of this unsightliness in a
few years when planted in the open. We offer
these in large quantities from new blocks, as-
suring their quality and vigor.

|  | Each | 10 |
|---|---|---|
| 12-14 feet | $2.50 | $20.00 |
| 10-12 feet | 2.00 | 17.50 |
| 8-10 feet | 1.50 | 12.50 |
| 7- 9 feet | 1.25 | 10.00 |

**Red Maple** (A. rubrum). If it were not for
the crooked trunks of this tree, as a lawn specimen it would prove most attractive. The
young shoots are bright red in winter, blooming
in early spring, a very brilliant color, with
pleasing foliage until frost. Then it vies with
the Oaks, Sassafras, Gum, Sumac or Sugar
Maples for magnificence in color. Used in
heavy border plantings to add character or
height; the effect must be seen to be appreciated.

|  | Each | 10 |
|---|---|---|
| 10-12 feet | $2.00 | $17.50 |
| 8-10 feet | 1.50 | 12.50 |

**Purple Leaved or Schwedler's Maple** (A.
Schwedleri). A tree resembling the Norway
Maple in every respect except in early spring
the foliage is a bright purple, gradually changing from bronze to dull green. In the fall it
turns bronze before defoliating.

|  | Each | 10 |
|---|---|---|
| 7-9 feet | $1.50 | $12.50 |
| 6-7 feet | 1.25 | 10.00 |

Pin Oak—Quercus Palustris.

durability not found in any other tree. It is the easiest of the oaks to transplant, more rapid of growth and in any capacity a tree may be used, whether shade, specimen, avenue, cemetery or park tree, if one is a little patient the reward is commensurate. So popular that we have nothing but the sizes as we list below to offer. Our block of several thousand trees has never been dug from before and our patrons will get only the most vigorous trees that will quickly establish themselves and grow off kindly.

|  | Each | 10 |
|---|---|---|
| 8-10 feet | $2.00 | $17.50 |
| 7- 9 feet | 1.50 | 12.50 |
| 6- 8 feet | 1.25 | 10.00 |

**Burr Oak** (Q. Macrocarpa). A native variety, of slower growth but in years a stately tree well covered with thick, dark green foliage of heavy texture. For permanency it has no superior. Prefers a moist or deep soil.

|  | Each | 10 |
|---|---|---|
| 10-12 feet | $2.00 | $17.50 |
| 8-10 feet | 1.75 | 15.00 |
| 6- 8 feet | 1.00 | 9.00 |

**Red Oak** (Q. rubra). Not as compact as Pin Oak, equally as rapid and a little more difficult to transplant, Red Oak is nevertheless very satisfactory. Leaves color purplish red in autumn and the tree will grow on any type of soil. Supply limited.

|  | Each | 10 |
|---|---|---|
| 8-10 feet | $1.50 | $12.50 |
| 7- 9 feet | 1.00 | 9.00 |

**Scarlet Oak** (Q. coccinea). So called because of its autumn coloring. Resembles Burr Oak in habits of growth.

|  | Each | 10 |
|---|---|---|
| 12-14 feet | $3.00 | $25.00 |
| 10-12 feet | 2.00 | 17.50 |
| 8-10 feet | 1.50 | 12.50 |

## Mulberry - Morus

**Russian Mulberry** (M. tartarica). This makes a round headed tree, quick of growth and very profuse foliage. It is wonderfully productive of fruit and for anyone wishing to attract birds this tree cannot be surpassed. If planted in chicken runs it will produce fruit for several months. The fruit is considerably smaller than our native variety but the tree bears so profusely that it is visible for a considerable distance.

|  | Each | 10 |
|---|---|---|
| 6-8 feet | $1.00 | $9.00 |

**Weeping Mulberry** (M. tartarica pendula). A very odd tree, immediately attractive with its long sweeping branches that touch the ground. It is grafted on its parent stock—Russian mulberry and is entirely free of all disease and bears shortly.

|  | Each | 10 |
|---|---|---|
| One year heads | $2.00 | $17.50 |

## Oak - Quercus

The derivation of the word literally means—fine trees. As a group there is nothing superior to the Oak. The tree while a little slow of growth, on well fertilized or naturally good soil is very quick to respond and the little extra effort that must be exercised to establish them is repaid. The shapeliness, the vigorous foliage, the hardihood and durability, toughness and color effect in autumn, make this a most interesting group.

**Pin Oak** (Q. palustris). Of all the oaks this is preferred. Perfectly symmetrical from the base branches up, foliage a shining green, leaves deeply cut and in the fall of wondrous colors—a combination for beauty, effect and

## Pecans

(See nut trees page 9.)

## Poplar - Populus

**Lombard Poplar** (P. fastigiata). A tall slender tree reaching great heights, very easy to transplant and of most rapid growth. Specimens often reach fifty feet with a spread of less than ten feet and for this reason when tree plantings are needed for narrow places, between buildings, congested lawns, narrow avenues, this may be used with great satisfaction. Because of its great height and quick growth it is commendable for backgrounds of buildings, to add character to plantings or to offset straight or bare lines. Further for screening unsightly views, fire protection from close buildings or wind breaks—and all for quick effect we unhesitatingly recommend this variety. A false impression prevails that it sheds its leaves early, but we assure of their misapprehension, as the tree is healthy in growth and foliage. Not the same as Carolina Poplar description which follows.

|  | Each | 10 |
|---|---|---|
| 10-12 feet | $1.50 | $12.50 |
| 8-10 feet | 1.00 | 9.00 |
| 7- 9 feet | .75 | 6.00 |

**Carolina Poplar** (P. monolifera). Once very popular for rapid growth and effect but so easily broken by wind and sleet, so prone to leaf rust, causing litter from June to frost that the public is warned against its planting.

**Tulip Poplar** (Liriodendron tulipifera). This is truly a magnolia and not a poplar. See Liriodendron for description and prices.

## Paulownia - Empress Tree

**Empress Tree** (P. imperialis). Very quick to establish, but sometimes freezes back in severe winters. Foliage conspicuous because of its abnormal size and the wood growth is very smooth. In bloom it resembles the catalpa somewhat but the color is purple. Unusual.

Extra heavy trees ...................$2.00

## Red Bud - Cercis

**Red Bud—Judas Tree** (C. canadensis). A native of our woods, literally covered with its red or pink blooms early in the spring before it opens its leaves. It is an early harbinger of spring, blooming in April. It is a small shapely tree, wood very tough and the leaves large and very dark green in color. It may be used in heavy mass planting of shrubs, with White Flowering Dogwoods or against evergreens or White Birch, in each case making a pleasant contrast.

|          | Each   | 10     |
|----------|--------|--------|
| 7-9 feet | $1.00  | $9.00  |
| 6-8 feet | .75    | 6.00   |
| 5-6 feet | .60    | 5.00   |

## Sycamore - Platanus

**American Sycamore or Plane Tree** (Platanus occidentalis). A native, sometimes thought too common to plant. However where a tree for quick effect is wanted, one clean in habit of growth, luxuriant of foliage and easy to transplant, this lesson of nature in distributing it so liberally should be accepted. The bark is silvery or grayish in winter, the leaves hold on well and for avenue, street, lawn and paddock shade, the Sycamore can be satisfactorily used.

|            | Each    | 10      |
|------------|---------|---------|
| 10-12 feet | $1.25   | $10.00  |
| 8-10 feet  | 1.00    | 10.00   |
| 7- 9 feet  | .75     | 6.00    |
| 6- 8 feet  | .60     | 5.00    |

## Walnut - Juglans

(See nut trees page 9.)

American Sycamore—Platanus Occidentalis

## Willow - Salix

**Weeping Willow** (S. Babylonica). A tree of stately appearance with long pendent branches swaying their silvery foliage in every breeze, quick to take hold when transplanted, will give a finish to a lawn not obtained in any other tree. This too makes a good screen and whether planted on moist or dry grounds thrives with unusual vigor.

|           | Each   | 10      |
|-----------|--------|---------|
| 8-10 feet | $1.25  | $10.00  |

# Shrubs For Special Purposes

### SHADE OR PARTIAL SHADE

| | |
|---|---|
| Mahonia | Weigelas |
| Abelia | Barberry |
| Hypericum | Deutzias |
| Snowberry | Forsythias |
| Coralberry | Snowballs |
| Hazelnut | Euonymus |
| Witch Hazel | Kerrias |
| Privets | |

### SHRUBS THAT COLOR IN FALL

| | |
|---|---|
| Cornelian Cherry | Witch Hazel |
| Holly-Leaved Barberry | Sumacs |
| Spirea prunifolia | Dogwood |
| High Bush Cranberry | Hawthorns |
| Common Barberry | Mahonia |
| Japan Barberry | Snowballs |
| Spindle Tree | |

### FOR WINTER EFFECT

| | |
|---|---|
| Snowberry | Kerria Japonica |
| Coralberry | Euonymus |
| High Bush Cranberry | Mahonia |
| Rosa Rugosa | Abelia |
| Red Twigged Dogwood | |

### BERRY-BEARING—ATTRACT BIRDS

| | |
|---|---|
| Service Berry | Buckthorn |
| Barberries | Sumac |
| Spindle Tree | Elder |
| Dogwood | Wayfaring Tree |
| Red Cedar | High Bush Cranberry |

Shrubs suitable for foundations designated by (F) in the descriptions.

**PRICES, EXCEPT AS NOTED, STRONG PLANTS, EACH, 50c; 10, $4.50; $40.00 PER 100. THOSE WANTING EXTRA HEAVY PLANTS ADD 10c ADDITIONAL TO ANY OF THESE LISTED KINDS STARRED *.**

# Deciduous Shrubs

The deciduous shrubs contain many interesting plants with foliage of various shades and blossoms of many colors. When planted as specimens and allowed to develop in symmetry and natural grace, shrubs do become objects of beauty. However, for softening the sharp angles or stiff lines of foundation walls or boundaries, screening of objectionable views, mass planting for effect or bringing out lawn features, or bordering the edges of walks, drives or boundaries, shrubs cannot be dispensed with in lawn ornamentation. Proper selection as to height and judicious choosing of varieties will insure the accomplishment of any of the mentioned objects and provide a succession of bloom from winter until fall.

Suggestions as to what you should plant for any particular plan, home or lawn will be cheerfully given. See page 1 for Shrubs for Special Purposes.

The blooming shrubs are better pruned immediately after flowering. The shortening of the tops in hedge fashion is wrong, but rather the thinning out of the older canes and branches, from the bottom is a better practice. Those that bloom on the terminal of the current year's growth, such as Hydrangeas, Hypericum, etc., are better pruned back severely each winter to insure vigorous shoots for the next season.

## Foundation Planting

Evergreens being rather expensive, many persons are planting the bare foundations with blooming shrubs. Those suitable for this purpose are marked (F)—and the height at maturity is designated in figures. A suggestion to obtain best effect—Plant the taller growing shrubs between the windows or in the corners and not under the windows as they will obstruct the view and ruin the natural planting effect desired. Massing of shrubs in the corners and angles is better practice than even spacing across the front. Use a double or staggered row in planting as this magnifies the effect and beauty. Where specimens are the tallest in the back row, the bed should be widest at that point. Shrubs reaching a height of six feet should be planted four feet apart, those maturing at five feet, should be set 3-3½ feet apart, etc., to obtain this massed effect. Such plantings of the home, are permanent improvements, a source of satisfaction to the owner, an object of beauty to the neighborhood.

Special attention is again called to our offer of "Home Grounds—Their Planning and Planting" on page 11.

We carry a wide assortment suitable for all purposes of ornamentation. Prices apply to best transplanting sizes of their respective kinds, the taller shrubs are usually sold in 3-5 foot sizes, and the dwarf varieties correspondingly smaller. We make shrubs a specialty, and offer only heavy plants.

## Abelia

Abelia (A. Grandiflora) (F). 2-3 ft. This is a new shrub. It is half hardy as in some severe winters it may be killed back to the crowns. This is not harmful to the vigor of the plant as it should be pruned every year, as it will push new shoots with renewed vigor, and as its beauty lies in its long arching branches, covered with small shining green leaves, a mass of white bell-shaped flowers borne in clusters, makes this pruning either by nature or with shears almost a requisite. To omit this pruning, your plants unless renewed from the base will become "top heavy" and lose the natural grace ever present in the young canes. Blooms in July and August, a period when good flowers are scarce. It is evergreen in mild winters and very distinct and unusual. Price for strong mature plants, 75 cents each.

## Amygdalus - Flowering Almond

Pink Flowering Almond (A. rosea flore pleno). This blooms in May, the branches being a mass of rose pink flowers, from the base to the tips of the branches. Plants are scarce, but to those knowing its beauty the extra price asked is very little. 75 cents each.

White Flowering Almond (A. alba pleno). Same as above save the flowers are white. Foliage of both varieties pleasing, and everyone should have a few plants among their shrubs.

## Amelanchier

*Amelanchier botryapium (Service Berry). 7-9 ft. Bush or small tree that is covered with clusters of small white flowers early in the spring before the foliage appears; valuable in background when massing shrubbery.

## Apple, Flowering Crab - Pyrus

Bechtel. Wonderful shell pink, double flowered, resembling a rose. Very fragrant. 3-4 ft. sizes. 75 cents each.

Flora bunda. Resembles the above, flower deeper in color. 75 cents each.

## Aralia - Angelica Tree

*A. pentaphylla (Five-leaved Aralia). 6-10 ft. A graceful shrub with arching, spiny branches and bright green leaves. Does well in rocky or sloping ground where other things are hard to establish.

A. spinosa (Hercules' Club). 7-10 ft. This grows to be a small tree, with long, spiny stem. Produces large panicles of white flowers late in summer. Foliage fern-like, spreading, and on the whole produces a very tropical appearance.

## Azalea

Azalea mollis. 18-24 in. A variety hardy here, though not especially vigorous grower, on our limestone soils. The blossoms are pink, very attractive in early spring before leaves are well grown. Price, $1.00 each.

## Berberis - Barberry

The Barberries are an interesting family of shrubs varying in size from 3 to 6 feet. Rich in variety of leaf, flower and fruit, and their beautiful colorings in the fall. Satisfactory for massing, bedding or as individuals.

Berberis illicifolia (Holly Leaved Barberry). (F). 3-4 ft. An upright growing shrub, with shining green leaves, terminal growth in early summer has a pleasing tint of color.

*B. Purpurea (Purple Leaved Barberry). 5-6 ft. (F). . One of the most attractive shrubs. The purple leaves appear in April, are so vivid and attractive, followed soon by their small yellow flowers, that it is surprising that more are not planted. The leaves hold their color all summer, followed by the usual attractive berries common to the barberries. For group or border planting or set against foundations you will find the effect most pleasing.

*B. Thunbergia (Japan Barberry). (F). 2½-3 ft. This variety hasn't a fault. A pretty species of dwarf, drooping habit that is used for outer border plantings and for hedges. It is perfectly hardy and will grow in partial shade, and endures drought well. The leaves turn a deep crimson in autumn, and when fallen the red berries are very showy. One of the most desirable shrubs we sell. Especially desirable for planting in front of foundations.

*B. Vulgaris (Common Barberry). 7-10 ft. Tall growing green leaf variety, to be used as backgrounds or in mass plantings. Foliage in fall is very brilliant, and this variety most productive of red berries that hang all winter.

## Butterfly Bush - Buddleia

Butterfly Bush or Summer Lilac (B. Veitchiana Magnifica). A very attractive new addition to the flowering plants. While a perennial in habit, yet because of its vigor and size, it is used largely in shrub plantings. The tops in severe winter will freeze back, but it pushes with such renewed vigor this is not harmful. The flowers are borne on the tips of every bit of new growth, and in August the plants are masses of purple and violet flowers very conspicuous. that attract butterflies. We recommend this.

Butterfly Bush—Buddleia.

## Calycanthus - Sweet Shrub

*C. Floridus (Allspice). This old-fashioned shrub is known to everyone. The flowers are not conspicuous but the fragrance makes it very popular. The foliage is free from disease, being glossy and hold well until late in the season.

## Cornus - Dogwood (Osiers)

C. Florida. White Flowering Dogwood. 15-20 ft. (See ornamentals page 13.)

*C. Sanguinea (European Red Osier). (F). 6-8 ft. A robust shrub that will grow where other varieties fail. Greenish-white flowers followed by clusters of small black berries. Twigs a dark red in winter.

*C. Siberica (Red Twigged Dogwood). 6-8 ft. Not so rank a grower as sanguinea, but the branches are of a bright red color in winter, showing for a great distance. Adds very much to shrubbery in the bleak, cold season.

*C. Mascula (Cornelian Cherry). 12-15 ft. A large growing shrub bearing clusters of bright yellow flowers before leaves appear in the spring. The berries are dark colored and the foliage in the fall is attractive. For erect hedges or screens this proves valuable or if planted as a specimen and kept well sheared proves attractive.

Elegantissima variegata. (F). 3-5 ft. A red bark variety also, but foliage is green, margined with white.

## Chionanthus - White Fringe

*C. virginica. 6-10 ft. Like the preceding, has been known for such a long period that description seems unnecessary. The foliage is very deep green, and when in bloom the mass of misty white blossoms against this foliage is most conspicuous. Not very rapid in growth yet as a single specimen or in groups proves worthy of the space occupied. 75 cents each.

Diervilla—Weigela.

## Cotoneaster

C. buxifolia. (F). 1-2 ft. A low, dwarf, spreading evergreen shrub with box-like leaves. White blossoms in spring, followed by red berries.

C. horizontalis. (F). Branches more horizontal than any other. Leaves small, glossy green, which remain all winter. White flowers followed by red berries.

C. macrophylla. (F). Leaves silvery-green, otherwise as preceding.

C. Simonsii. 2 ft. Semi-evergreen shrub; dark shiny leaves during the summer; which turn red late in the fall; white flowers followed by red berries.

All varieties, 75 cents each.

## Crataegus - Hawthorn

*C. Crus-Galli (Cockspur Thorn). Like the native shrubs, thorny, but a mass of white flowers in spring, followed by brilliantly colored fruit and highly colored orange and red foliage during the autumn months.

## Deutzia

A Japan shrub noted for its hardiness, fine habit, luxuriant foliage and profusion of attractive flowers which are borne in racemes during June. The small florets are similar to Lily-of-the-Valley.

*D. candidissima. (F). 6-8 ft. A pleasing white; free bloomer.

*D. gracilis. (F). 1½-2 ft. A charming dwarf shrub, growing to a height of 2 to 3 feet; blooms abundantly.

*D. Lemoinei. (F). 2½-3 ft. Another dwarf grower with pure white flowers; blossoms early.

*D. Pride of Rochester. (F). 6-8 ft. Flowers purplish-white with the under side of petals tinged rose.

## Diervilla - The Weigelas

An important genus from Japan that is almost indispensable for ornamental planting. They will thrive in any soil and in partial shade. When young they are more upright, but when older become more graceful. They produce a wealth of bell-shaped blossoms along the branches in June and often sparingly during the summer.

*W. candida. (F). 5-6 ft. Upright; strong; the old pure white.

*W. Eva Rathke. (F). 3½-4 ft. Of slower and more spreading growth than other Weigelas. The dark red flowers are produced later than the others. Very showy.

*W. rosea. (F). 4-5 ft. Delicate pink and sometimes rose, often fading to almost white. One of the best.

## Euonymus - Spindle Tree

E. Europeus. 8-10 ft. Grows to be a small tree, 25 to 30 feet. Has smooth branches and small white flowers. It is especially desirable because of its white and rose-colored fruit in fall. The leaves are a brilliant scarlet in autumn, and together with the fruit make a handsome appearance.

## Forsythia - Golden Bell

Pretty shrubs of medium size, blooming in spring before leaves appear. Flowers are yellow, drooping, and are borne along the stem. They are exceptionally hardy and thrive in any locality. The green branches also add to their attractiveness, and the graceful bushy or pendulous habit.

F. suspensa. 3-4 ft. A drooping variety that makes a desirable bush when planted alone or can be made to arch trellises, etc.

*F. Fortunei. (F). 6-10 ft. A form of suspensa, but with more upright branches and darker, heavier foliage.

*F. viridissima. 6-8 ft. The most popular of all. Branches a bright green even in winter; blooms profusely. Foliage rather long, pointed and glossy.

## Hydrangea

No class of shrubs are better known than the Hydrangeas, as they include some of the most showy plants in cultivation. Transplant easily, have no diseases, and bloom in the fall when there is a scarcity of flowers. We only have the hardy varieties.

H. arborescens grandiflora. (F). 3-4 ft. (Also Hills of Snow, Summer Hydrangea, or Snowball Hydrangea). This magnificent hardy American shrub is the very finest addition to this class of plants found in many a year. The blooms are of the very largest size, of pure snow-white color and the foliage is finely finished. One of its most valuable characteristics is its coming into bloom just after the passing of the early spring shrubs, while its long period of bloom—from early June through August—makes it doubly valuable, not only to the florist, but to every owner of a garden. Perfectly hardy. Habit of plant excellent.

H. paniculata grandiflora. (F). 4-5 feet. (Great Panicled Hydrangea). Commonly known as hardy Hydrangea. This popular variety does not bloom until August and September. The large spikes are first greenish-white then pure white, later changing to bronze pink.

## Halesia - Silver Bell

*H. Tetraptera (Silver Bell). 15-20 ft. A rather large shrub or small tree that is loaded with white snowdrop-like flowers in spring. Does well in shady places.

## Hamamelis - Witch Hazel

*H. virginiana (Witch Hazel). In late fall has a wealth of small yellow flowers coming at a season when nothing else is in bloom. For natural plantings it is especially recommended. Foliage is bright green until changed to yellow and orange after frost.

## Hibiscus - Althea - Rose of Sharon

(F). 6-10 ft. Free growing shrubs that are especially desirable because they bloom at a time of the year when there are few flowers, July and August. Valuable for a flowering hedge to hide an undesirable background—or as individual specimens.

The flowers come in many shades and we catalog them to color. White, Purple, and Red.

## Hypericum - St. John's Wort

H. moserianum. (F). 1-2 ft. This rather unique low-growing shrub always attracts attention. Flower a beautiful rich yellow, borne on slender stems, surrounded with rather roundish, leathery green leaves throughout the summer. During severe winters it often kills to the ground but next spring will come back more vigorous than before.

## Kerria - Corchorus

K. Japonica. (F). 3-4 ft. Slender shrub, stoloniferous, with bright green branches, which remain so during winter. Foliage a deep green forming a pleasing background for the single yellow flowers that come throughout the summer months.

K. Japonica flore-pleno. (F). Identical to above, save globe-shaped double flowers from July to October.

## Lonicera - Honeysuckles

The honeysuckle family is a varied one, including vines and shrubs. The former is included under "Climbing Vines." The bush varieties are in demand, though not planted as they should be. They transplant easily, grow rapidly, have fragrant flowers and almost all are followed by brilliant red fruit. Desirable for individual or mass planting.

L. fragrantissima. (F). 6-8 ft. A sweet scented variety that blooms before the foliage expands in early spring. Flowers are creamy-white; leaves a deep green, which is retained until midwinter. This variety will adapt itself to any soil, grows vigorously, and is perhaps the favorite of the shrub Honeysuckles. For screening, as in mild winters, it holds its foliage the entire season.

L. Morrowi. 8-10 ft. A Japanese variety of robust, spreading character, of excellent foliage and branched in such a manner that it appears a perfect bank of green. The flowers are white, fragrant, and these are followed by brilliant red, and sometimes coral colored berries, scattered through the foliage and remaining all summer, making this variety a most popular one. Easy to transplant and like the family will do well on any soil.

L. Tartarica (Rubra). 6-8 ft. An old-fashioned shrub of rather upright form with pink or crimson blushed flowers. Foliage a lively green. The flowers and foliage enmassed make this one of the most sought after kinds.

L. Tartarica (Alba). 6-8 ft. A form of the Rubra, similar except the flowers are pure white.

Lonicera Morrowi—Bush Honeysuckle.

## Ligustrum - Privet

A group of ornamental shrubs most desirable for landscape work, and often lost sight of because they are thought of as hedge plants only. Not particular about soil, and grow well in partial shade. They have bright green leaves which remain on well and are seldom attacked by insects.

*L. amurense (Amoor River Privet). (F). 6-10 ft. A small leaf, almost evergreen variety of Privet that is much used for hedges. Desirable to give body to mass planting of shrubbery or as individual specimens.

L. ovalifolium (California Privet). 6-10 ft. This we grow in quantity for hedge, but as an individual plant few excel it either in wealth of creamy flowers or exquisite beauty of form and foliage. Semi-evergreen. See hedge plants.

*L. regelianum (Regel's Privet). (F). 5-7 ft. A low, spreading variety, being very twiggy, with a dense foliage not so glossy as California. Because of its graceful appearance, hardiness and adaptability to any soil, and shady places, it is the most widely used Privet for landscape work.

## Magnolia

M. Soulangeana. 7-8 ft. This beautiful shrub opens its white, purple striped cup-shaped flowers early in spring before the leaves appear. An elegant, showy shrub. $1.25 each.

M. Kobus. 10-15 ft. Branches from ground up, shining leaves and very hardy. White, fragrant flowers in early spring. For a flowering tree unsurpassed. $1.25 each.

Magnolia Grandiflora. This is the Southern Evergreen Magnolia; very popular but exceedingly difficult to grow on limestone soils. We do not recommend it except to persons that are willing to give them special attention in establishing. The flowers are white, very fragrant and the leaves are very large, leathery and bright green, remaining all winter. 4-5 foot trees at $1.25 each.

Mock Orange—Philadelphus.

## Mahonia - Ashberry

**M. aquifolia.** (F). 2-3 ft. Holly leaf Mahonia. Its shining, dark green, prickly foliage, yellow flowers in early spring, which turn a bright bronze in winter, and the fact that it will thrive under trees in the shade make it popular. An evergreen that is useful to plant with other shrubs or along foundations. In planting clip off all the leaves and much better results will be obtained in getting them to live. As the new growth appears for the first year or so, if after two or three leaves are formed one will pinch off the canes this will make the plants bushy and increase the size of the foliage. Plants **18** inches, 75 cents each.

## Philadelphus

### Mock Orange or Syringa

A tall, vigorous and hardy bush. It bears profuse white flowers resembling orange blossoms. These shrubs are very valuable for backgrounds, screens, grouping or specimen plants. The beautiful white flowers are fine for cutting.

*P. coronarius.** (F). 6-8 ft. The old-fashioned mock orange, known to everyone because of its early, white, fragrant flowers. The bush is a model of vigor.

*P. grandiflora.** 7-10 ft. A French variety conspicuous because of its large flowers. Blooms later than the above.

P. Lemoinei erectus.** (F). 4-5 feet. A slender, erect growing type, with creamy white flowers that almost cover the bush.

## Pyrus or Cydonia

**Pyrus Japonica** (Japan Quince). 6-8 feet. The most beautiful of early blooming shrubs, and as a mass of scarlet or crimson, tinged in the exquisite green of its glossy foliage, it has no rival.

## Rhamnus

*R. catharticus** (Buckthorn). 12-16 ft. A hardy shrub for poor soils, exposed and neglected places. Also desirable for a rough hedge, having a few thorns and almost impenetrable. The berries are a mecca to the birds and planted for this purpose they will attract them quickly.

## Rhodotypos

*R. kerrioides** (White Kerria). (F). 5-6 ft. A very ornamental-shrub with handsome pleated leaves and large white flowers late in May, succeeded by small fruit. Desirable.

## Rhus - Sumac

The Sumacs as a class appeal to the planter most for the wonderful fall coloring of the foliage.

*R. cotinus** (Purple Fringe). 12-16 ft. Better known as Smoke Tree. When loaded with its great gaudy spikes no shrub is more beautiful, and even when ripe are very attractive. **75 cents each.**

*R. glabra** (Smooth Sumac). 10-15 ft. One of the best of the Sumacs to produce natural effects.

R. laciniata.** 8-10 ft. A cut-leaf form of the above that looks like a fern, tropical in appearance and showy.

*R. typhina** (Staghorn Sumac). 10-12 ft. A large shrub or tree much used in landscape background work. Brilliant red foliage in the fall.

## Rosa Rugosa

A Japanese form, with large, thick, glossy leaves and large, single red flowers; very striking as a shrub and especially desirable for massing. (F). 5-6 ft.*

## Sambucus - Elder

*S. nigra** (Black Elder). These shrubs prove valuable not alone for their foliage but for blossom and berries. These latter ripen in August and attract the birds in great numbers. Easy to transplant and grow rapidly.

## Stephanandra

S. flexuosa.** (F). 2-3 ft. A thick shrub with small, slender, rather drooping branches; light green, fern-like leaves which turn a bronze in the fall. Small, inconspicuous blooms during summer. A pretty shrub that is not used enough.

## Symphoricarpos

S. racemosus** (Snowberry). (F). 4-5 feet. This shrub has small, pinkish flowers in July, followed by white berries which remain on well into the winter.

S. vulgaris** (Coralberry or Buck Bush). 4-5 feet. A very hard, tough shrub that can be established where others fail. Its wealth of coral-like red berries are quite showy during winter. This and the Snowberry go well together.

**Spirea Van Houttei.**

## Spirea - Meadow Sweet

We know of no family of shrubs that are quite so popular. They bloom from earliest to latest and our stock is large and complete.

**S. Anthony Waterer.** (F.)   2 ft.   A small dwarf variety 1½ feet, covered with flat heads of pink flowers.   Used for edging and in front of shrubbery.

**S. callosa rosea.** (F.)   3 ft.   Has large panicles of deep rosy blossoms.   Grows freely and blooms most of the summer.   Resembles the dwarf variety S. Anthony Waterer.

**\*S. Billardi rosea.** 5-6 ft.   Erect branches crowned with narrow dense spikes of rose-colored flowers.

**S. Douglasii.** 6-7 ft.   Cone-shaped flowers in July and August of bright rose color and blooming over a long period.   This variety grows erect and is popular.

**\*S. prunifolia** (Bridal Wreath). (F.)   5-6 ft. Flowers white, early and very double.   Foliage turns bronze in autumn.

**S. Thunbergii** (Snow Garland). (F.)   2-3 ft. An extra early flowering type of graceful form. Leaves light green, drooping; flowers white; rather dwarf, but desirable.   Fine for bordering.

**\*S. Reevesii.** (F.)   A charming variety with graceful branches and rather long cut-leaf foliage; blossoms in white clusters over the whole plant.

**S. Van Houttei** (Bridal Bower). (F.)   4-6 feet.   This shrub is so popular that we sell more of it than any other variety we grow.   It blooms in May and the pendent branches sometimes drooping to the ground are a mass of white.   The foliage is an attractive green, which it retains late in the year.   This shrub is so meritorious that its uses are unlimited. Its profusion of blossom, its health of foliage, its graceful form, its adaptability to soils and purposes make it deservedly popular.   We recommend it most highly.

## Syringa - The Lilacs

No shrubs are better known or more deservedly popular than the lilac.   Besides the old-fashioned kinds we are offering budded varieties that are in many ways superior to the old-fashioned ones; all of the named sorts are double.

**Lilac** (Persian).   6-8 feet. Small foliage and bright purple flowers.

**\*Lilac** (Purple).   7-10 feet. The well-known old-fashioned variety with purple fragrant flowers in May.

**\*Lilac** (White).   6-8 feet. Same as the above but with white blossoms.

## Tamarix

Shrubs of strong but slender, delicate growth similar to the asparagus.   The pink flowers, filmy foliage and gracefulness make them one of the most desirable shrubs for a background or inter-planting. Will grow in poor, dry soil where other shrubs fail.

**A. aestivalis.** (F.)   6-7 ft.   This species has bluish-gray foliage, carmine pink flowers, and blooms late in the summer.

**T. Africana.**   7-10 ft.   This is the most vigorous of any.   Sea green foliage and pink flowers; blooms early.

## Viburnum - The Snowballs

In this group are some of the most conspicuous shrubs for blossom, berries or autumnal foliage we have.   They are all hardy, vigorous and healthy.   For individual specimens or shrubbery borders they are desirable.   Most of them will grow in a partial shade but do better in the sun.

**\*V. lantana** (Wayfaring Tree). (F.)   10-12 ft.   A large, vigorous shrub with soft, heavy, lantana-like leaves and large clusters of white flowers in May, succeeded by red berries which turn black as they ripen.

**\*V. opulus** (High Bush Cranberry).   8-10 ft. Strong, rather spreading habit with single white flowers borne in flat clusters.   The very showy red fruit which follows and the beautiful coloring in the fall go to make it one of the best.

**V. plicatum** (Japanese Snowball).   6-8 feet. This species is one of the most satisfactory shrubs grown.   Its pure white double blossoms with a setting of dark pleated leaves and perfect form make it one of the best.   Fine for an individual specimen or in groups.

**\*V. sterilis** (Old-Fashioned Snowball).   10-12 ft.   This old-fashioned variety is well known to every lover of plants.   Its balls of pure white, literally cover the bush when in bloom.

**\*V. tomentosum.** (F.)   6-8 ft.   The single form of Japanese Snowball; equally desirable.

## Xanthorrhiza

**X. Sorbifolia** (Ash Leaved Spirea).   Blooms in July in long white spikes.   Foliage resembles an ash somewhat.   Valued for shady or moist locations.

---

**PRICES OF ALL SHRUBS, EXCEPT AS NOTED, 50c EACH, $4.50 PER 10, $40.00 PER 100.   EXTRA LARGE SPECIMENS IN VARIETIES STARRED (\*) 10c ADDITIONAL.**

California Privet Hedge.

# Hedge Plants

A living fence—one made of plants, attractive with their green leaves, formal trained or arched branches, colored foliage or bright berries is surely more pleasing that the still, rigid, mechanical effect obtained by the similar use of wood or metal. A lawn hedge is permanent— once planted, only occasional pruning or shearing is required. It is better practice in pruning to round the top than to shear perfectly flat on top, as this gives the bottom and side branches an opportunity to reach the sunlight and air necessary for full development of the hedge at its base and near the ground line. Hedges pruned square on top simply form a shade for these lower branches, which soon become weak in growth, and the hedge row becomes unsightly because of the meagre foliage near its base. Hedges of flowering plants should never be pruned formal, but allowed to develop naturally, sneaking out only occasional canes that are ungainly.

For hedges you may use a variety of plants, including not only the privets and barberries, but flowering shrubs like Hydrangeas, Purple-leaved Barberries, Altheas, Spireas, Fragrant Bush Honeysuckle, Evergreens, in fact any of the compact growing shrubs may be used. Prices on these will be quoted on application.

Distances Apart to Plant—Privet, 8-10 inches; Japan Barberry, 12 inches; Flowering Shrubs 2-2½ feet; Norway Spruce, 3-6 feet.

## California Privet

A semi-evergreen hedge with thick, shining leather leaves, that grows very quickly, can be pruned into any formal effect and planted by everyone needing a quick hedge without much expense or trouble. It blossoms in spring, the fragrant white flowers being noticeable for some distance. In planting it is a good idea to cut away practically all the tops of the smaller plants in order to get a bushy hedge. Prune severely leaving only 5-6 inches of wood remaining. We have quantities of this desirable variety.

|  | 100 | 1,000 |
|---|---|---|
| 1 year, 12-18 inch | $3.00 | $25.00 |
| 1 year, 18-24 inch | 4.00 | 35.00 |
| 2 year, 2-3 feet | 5.00 | 40.00 |
| 2 year, 3-4 feet | 6.00 | 50.00 |

## Norway Spruce

For an evergreen hedge, absolute screen of objectionable views or wind break, winter or summer, this is the most desirable evergreen for the purpose, known. They may be planted 3-6 feet apart, depending on the compactness of the resultant hedge desired. These trees may be sheared in any conceivable manner. responding to pruning very kindly. The specimens we offer have been transplanted, and have good root systems. If in need of an evergreen hedge try some of our trees.

|  | 10 | 100 |
|---|---|---|
| 3-4 feet | $6.00 | $50.00 |
| 4-5 feet | 7.50 | 60.00 |

## Berberis Thunbergii

This Japanese shrub is being used more and more as a hedge. Not as quick in growth as C. Privet, but absolutely hardy. Its small, glossy leaves are out early in spring, succeeded by yellow flowers. The foliage turns a bright red in the fall, and this is followed by red berries. It is a graceful, drooping shrub, making an elegant variety for hiding foundation walls or planting in the corners by steps, etc., also does well in shady places. Especially remarkable for its brilliant red berries, remaining fresh until spring, and for its dazzling fall coloring. Our heavier bushy plants will make immediate effect when planted.

|  | 10 | 100 | 1,000 |
|---|---|---|---|
| 15 to 18 inches | $2.00 | $15.00 | $150.00 |
| 18 to 24 inches | 3.00 | 20.00 | 175.00 |

## Other Hedge Plants

Regal's Privet  
Common Barberry  
Cornelian Cherry  
Hydrangeas  
Fragrant Bush Honey-  
suckle  

Snowballs, etc.  
Amoor River Privet  
Purple Barberry  
Deutzias  
Altheas  
Spireas  

Prices on application.

Hall's Honeysuckle—Lonicera.

# Climbing and Clinging Vines

With their variance in color, their beauty of foliage and blossom, their grace wherever used, these vines frequently provide the finishing touches of any planting.  Some adhere to the masonry, some must be trained through lattice or trellis and others with their tendrils will cling tenaciously, unshaken by wind or weather.  Visualize the effect desired and train them accordingly to cover your walls and pilasters, your lattice or trellis, the pergola or laundry posts, the porch or portico, veranda or on the fence for shade, grace or flower and let them ramble in their plentitude—objects of beauty and a pleasure to the planter.

PRICES, EXCEPTIONS NOTED, EACH 40 CENTS, $3.00 PER 10.

## Ampelopsis

A. quinquefolia (Virginia Creeper).  Valuable for covering old fences, etc.  Leaves red in fall.

A. veitchii (Boston Ivy).  The beautiful self-clinging vine that is used to cover walls of stone or brick.  Leaves form a dense sheet of green as they overlap each other; a little difficult to start, but when once established requires no further care.  Foliage changes to a crimson-scarlet in the fall.

## Clematis Hybrids

These popular vines are known and planted everywhere for the profusion of beautiful, large flowers they produce.  Not as hardy or healthy as C. paniculata, but when once established are worthy of all the extra care in getting them started.

C. Jackmanii.  Large, purple. ⎫
C. Andre.  Large red.             ⎬ 50c each.
C. Henryii.  Large white.         ⎭
We import our stock of these. ⎭

C. Paniculata.  The small white, sweet-scented varieties that are beautiful both in foliage and blossom.  40c each.

ROSES—See page 26.

## Trumpet Vine - Bignonia

A robust, woody vine, twining tightly with numerous tendrils along its stems.  Leaves are dark green.  Very desirable for covering summer houses, arbors, trees or rustic bridges.

B. radicans.  The most familiar variety, with its scarlet flowers.  Native.

B. grandiflora.  Earlier and larger than B. radicans, the flowers are a beautiful orange red.

## Wistaria

A rampant clinging vine that has the robust vigor of a wild grape and the matchless beauty of a rare exotic.  Colors both white and purple.

Euonymus radicans.  A slow growing vine, that adheres to the masonry and remains deep green all winter.  For tall foundations and where only a small vine is wanted this will be excellent.

E. radicans variegata.  Same as above except the foliage is margined with white; on dark walls this proves as effective as the above.

## Honeysuckle - Lonicera

Hall's.  This is the popular evergreen honeysuckle, used by everyone for screen, beauty and fragrance.  Blooms continuously and easy to establish.  It is also evergreen, holding its foliage all winter.

Coral Honeysuckle.  Flowers bright scarlet, little fragrance but is strong grower and hardy.

Ampelopsis Veitchii—Boston Ivy.

White Cochet Roses.

# Roses

. The most popular flower known today. The gardens of our grandmothers were wonderful in June, but after years of careful breeding, experimenting and testing, we have hundreds of varieties that give us a wealth of bloom throughout the summer and until frost. Hardly a home is complete without a few plants. The bush roses may be used anywhere a foliage or blooming plant could be, and the wonderful climbing varieties in their colors may be left alone to ramble over the fences, along the embankments for ground covers, drooping over walls or abutments or trained over trellis, lawn benches or twined about the pillars of the veranda.

Planted in soils that are deep and rich, in the open sunlight they produce their best flowers. The everblooming varieties, are hardy usually, yet in some winters of abnormal temperature they will injure, and for this reason we advise some protection with straw, manure, leaves or soil about them—takes but little time, oft repaid in the pleasure the flowers afford.

In planting prune them back to three or four good buds, as they will grow off much better. The everblooming roses should be shortened back each year about one-half the previous season's growth. The ramblers may be pruned by taking out the older canes after they are through blooming and removing the flower spikes, leaving only the younger cane. Budded roses should be planted deeper to cover the offset or crook just above the soil mark on the plant. Our plants are mostly own-root and field-grown and not the small pot roses usually offered.

|  | Each | 10 |
|---|---|---|
| Field Grown Plants .................................................. | $0.60 | $5.00 |

## Everbloomers or Monthly

### WHITE ROSES

**Clothilde Soupert.** A strong dwarf grower that is unsurpassed for bedding. White, shading to a deep pink at the center; fragrant.

**Druschki, Snow Queen.** Vigorous grower, producing large, pure white blossoms. Considered by many as the best white rose in existence.

**Sir Thomas Lipton.** The best pure white Rugosa rose. Strong and vigorous. Flowers perfectly double and snow white. Absolutely hardy everywhere.

**White Cochet.** A most beautiful rose in bud, and equally so when expanded. Pure white at center, with the outer petals tinged with pink. We consider it the best.

### RED OR CRIMSON

**Eugene Marlet.** Bright red changing to crimson. Fine.

**General Jacqueminot.** A most popular, rich, red rose, known and wanted by everyone.

### PINK ROSES

**Conrad Meyer.** Another rose with the hardy Rugosa blood in it. Color deep pink, healthy, vigorous and considered one of the best. Awarded many first medals at rose societies in both countries.

**Hermosa.** An everblooming, hardy, beautiful rose. Popular for many years. Deep pink.

**Paul Neyron.** One of the largest roses grown. Color a clear rose pink and by some called the pink American Beauty, which it resembles much in form and color. Has few thorns.

**Pink Cochet.** We consider it one of the best pink roses. Beautiful at all times and a free bloomer. It won't disappoint.

**Mrs. Cant.** The clear, bright red, pointed buds, when opened are extra full, changing to rare pink. A profuse bloomer and excellent for cutting.

## Climbing Roses

**American Pillar.** Flowers large and single; range from 2 to 3 inches. Brilliant carmine-rose with cream variations and yellow stamens at center; produced in immense clusters, being very showy and attractive. Unquestionably one of the finest single climbing Roses known. Strong, rapid growth, healthy foliage and a wealth of flowers.

**Climbing American Beauty.** This is a seedling of the well known American Beauty, which it resembles in size and color of blossoms and in addition has the climbing habit. We have not grown it extensively, but everywhere it is fast becoming popular.

**Crimson Rambler.** Bright crimson flowers produced in large clusters. We like Excelsa better.

**Dorothy Perkins.** A most beautiful deep pink. Flowers are borne in large clusters and are fragrant. The climbing rose for the masses. We grow them by the thousands, more than all the other climbers combined.

**Dr. W. Van Fleet.** Out of our many test kinds this stood out prominently. Its soft pink, fragrant flowers are borne on long, stiff stems, and for cutting is equal to any rose grown.

**Excelsa or Red Dorothy.** A new climbing rose that truly may be called a "brilliant Crimson Rambler." Foliage glossy and healthy. Superior to Crimson Rambler.

**Silver Moon.** A new rose, of deep glossy green foliage, flowers being very large white with yellow stamens. Hardy and vigorous.

Hardy Perennial Border.

# Hardy Perennials

For permanent planting, for variance, beauty of flower effect and pleasure, the perennial plants offer a field from which one may select in color, or in period of bloom, plants to suit the tastes of the most fastidious.  Our list includes only the most desirable ones.    There are hundreds of varieties and kinds, many are meritorious, but for the average bed, group or border, one will find the selection that follows, suitable to ordinary purposes.

May it be said that these plants thrive better in fertile ground, and plenty of moisture, should be well cultivated and kept free of weeds for best results.  For the sake of neatness after the blooming period the flower stems should in part be cut out, being careful to leave sufficient foliage to conduct the natural functions of the plant.  Some perennials become sluggish and often revert to parent or unsightly colors, and this pruning defeats nature's purpose of producing seed, therefore conserving the strength of the plant and later results in better bloom.

Ordinarily perennials are set 18 inches apart for the larger growing and 15 inches for the dwarf plants.  In planning a border, if one will mark his rows going each way so as to make squares the number of plants is quickly ascertained, the arrangement as to height is easily arrived at and the grouping or planting made easy by alternating or varying a few inches from these rigid lines.  Mulching for winter protection is necessary, care must be taken not to smother the plants by covering the crowns.  Bulbs that are hardy may be scattered through such a border and after blooming remove their tops and in their places plant a few good annuals, the color and beauty of the border will be accentuated and the care and upkeep not increased.

PRICES, EXCEPTIONS NOTED, 25c EACH, $2.00 PER 10, $15.00 PER 100.

## Achillea - Yarrow or Milfoil

A. Boule de Neige (Ball of Snow).  2 feet.  A mass of pure white double flowers coming in July and blooming for a long period.  For mass effect or for cutting it is valuable.

## Aquilegias - Columbines

Blooming in late spring and through the early summer months, preferring slightly shaded positions, though it does well in the sun.  The flowers are borne on slender stems and mostly long spurred—coming in the many shades they do, prove very valuable in any border.  2-3 feet.

## Asters - Michaelmas Daisies

Blooming in September and October, and being hardy they are very popular.  Colors are pink, purple and white.  3-4½ feet.  Should be in every border.

## Buddleia - Butterfly

(See shrubs page 19.)

## Chrysanthemums

These are hardy and most attractive in September and October.  In planting these try to group them as some seasons it may be necessary to save from early frost by covering with sheets.  Height 2-3 feet.  The flowers are very attractive, borne in large quantities, the bushes being a mass of blossoms. Colors, White, Pink, Red and Yellow.

## Coreopsis

A beautiful yellow flower, desirable for cutting or for border.  Blooms in June, flowers being two inches across when well grown.  After blooming the tops may be cut away and a good secondary blossoming will follow all through the summer.  The best yellow flower for the border.  Height 2-3 feet.  Graceful.

I have been very much pleased with your evergreens. I have had better success with mine than any of my neighbors, who purchased elsewhere.—Mrs. J. P. C., Richmond, Ky.

Delphinium—Larkspur.

## Delphiniums

A blue flower, whose praises have been sung by every lover of a hardy border. The flowers are borne in great spikes, the first coming about the first of June. These may be cut away and young growth will start from the crown producing some bloom all through the summer. Height, 3-4 feet. Mulch lightly as the crowns sometimes rot over winter.

**Belladonna.** Light turquoise blue, the most continuous bloomer of the two varieties.

**Formosum.** The deep or dark blue, lighter centers and a robust grower. The best of the dark shades.

## Hardy Grasses

This group contains very valuable plants for beds and borders, parks or cemeteries, under trees or alongside of lakes or ponds. They are very effective. Because they do not produce highly colored flowers but filmy spikes or plumes they have been neglected. Their ease of transplanting, freedom of disease, and the grace of their falling blades should be points in their favor.

**Arundo donax** (Giant Reed). This variety grows to a height of 12 to 15 feet, and is especially desirable for background, the central feature of a bed planted with grasses, or to screen undesirable outlooks. Its long drooping bright narrow green leaves resemble a healthy stalk of corn though more artistic.

**Eulalia Japonica.** 5-6 feet. A hardy grass of robust growth and light green leaves. Used largely for backgrounds or centers of beds.

**Eulalia Gracillima.** 3-4 feet. This is the most graceful of the grasses, and therefore most popular. For individual or mass planting it is unexcelled. By all means plant some of this variety if interested in any of the grasses.

**Eulalia zebrina.** Similar to Japonica, being, as the name indicates cross striped with white. This is very pretty.

## Gaillardia - Blanket Flower

Will grow anywhere, bearing large quantities of yellow flowers flecked and marked with crimson and brown. Starting in June, there are blossoms all summer. One of the most desirable plants for the home garden as the flowers are valued for cutting.

## Helianthus - Sunflower

**Miss Mellish.** A beautiful yellow, blooming in August, flowers being 2 inches across and on strong stems. The flowers are single and the foliage free of disease. Spreads quickly and produces tall stalks 5-7 feet. Valued for its period of bloom and height.

## Hibiscus - Mallow

A fine plant, producing single bell-shaped flowers, frequently 4-6 inches across, and blooming over a long period. The bush attains a height of 5 feet and is perfectly hardy. Valuable acquisition to the perennials. Flowers borne in July and August. Pink and white.

## Hollyhocks

Everyone knows them—with their long spikes of multi-colored flowers, borne in profusion as they are, there is no wonder they are so largely used. Blooming in June and July, so absolutely hardy that they will take care of themselves.

**Single Hollyhocks.** 5-6 feet. These are seedlings, grown from the very best plants of senator J. N. Camden's gardens, and anyone who has seen them in bloom there, knows their wonderful beauty.

**Double Hollyhock.** 4 feet. This is a strain of double Hollyhock, from imported stock. Color a decided coral, shading to light pink on the edge of the petals and the flowers are borne in great profusion from base to tips of stalks. Blossoms fringed or very double.

Gaillardia—Blanket Flower.

PRICES, 25c EACH, $2.00 PER 10, $15.00 PER 100.  NOTE EXCEPTIONS.

# Iris

There is a peculiar charm about the Iris that appeals irresistibly to those whose taste for the refined and delicately beautiful, leads them to seek a closer acquaintance with it. Its iridescent coloring, fragile, orchid-like formation is often unnoticed by the careless observer. But those who only know the Iris as "flags" have never really examined "the rainbow flower," "messengers from the Queen of Heaven to mortals on earth." We want you to plant some of them, especially the Japanese variety, and see that one investment means years of beauty. Cultivation is simple. They do not need to be replanted each year, and will last indefinitely when once established.

These are the old-fashioned flags, and the varieties we offer are exceptionally meritorious, being selected for variety and distinct coloring. 25 cents each; $2.00 per 10.

## Liberty Iris

**Black Prince.** Standards deep violet-blue, falls purple.

**Florentina alba.** Standards and falls white, tinged with yellow and blue.

**Honorabilis.** Standards golden yellow, falls rich mahogany brown.

**Pallida dalmatica.** A tall variety. Lavender shading to blue.

**Spectabilis.** Standards pale lavender, falls blue and old gold.

**Queen of May.** A soft rose-lilac, almost pink.

**Walneri.** Standards lavender, falls a purple-lilac.

## Japanese Iris

This is the latest blooming of the Iris. Anyone not familiar with these has missed one of the glories of the garden. They bloom in June, being the largest, showiest and contain varieties that for variance of color and beauty are unsurpassed by any perennial. Prefers moist soil, but blooms exceedingly well on any type. 25 cents each; $2.00 per 10.

You may order by number.

**Shigano Uranami (11).** Double. Extra large lavender, minutely veined white. Early.

**Idzumi Gawa (12).** Double. A beautiful gray shaded and veined blue.

**Kurokumo (13).** Double. A very deep blue with lighter markings.

**Furomon (14).** Double. An excellent early white, bordered and laced pink.

**Geishoni (15).** Double. Royal purple, shaded crimson. Very late.

## Monarda - Cambridge Scarlet or Bergamot

A very brilliant colored flower, unusual and attractive, coming in July and if the old blossoms are pinched out there will be a continuous bloom until fall. Succeeds everywhere, and should be in every border. The foliage if crushed is aromatic, reminding one of mint. Grows 2½-3 feet.

Iris Florentina Alba.

## Phlox

Nothing grows in the perennial class that is as satisfactory as the Hardy Phloxes. They are wonderful in their many shades, their profusion of bloom and general good character. Our list is not large but the very best varieties of their respective shades from a test row of many kinds. It is a good idea to break out the flowering spikes after they have finished blooming. Root prune or transplant every few years. (We mark them without prefix of Lords and Lassies).

**(Sir Edward) Landseer.** A brilliant pleasing shade of salmon-red, very striking.

**(Frau G. Von) Lassburg.** A late white, producing great spikes or trusses of pure white flowers. Fine.

**(Miss) Lingard.** Another white but blooms in April. Removing the seed spikes a good second bloom is to be had. Best white known. Early.

**Pantheon.** Just as soft, pleasing shade of rose-pink as could be had in a Phlox. Blooms in July and very fine.

**(Sir Richard) Wallace.** Vigorous grower and pronounced the best of its season. White with violet center. Attractive.

## Poppies

These are Oriental Poppies, vivid shade of red, blooming with the peonies and the joy and admiration of everyone. Plant a few of our divisions and have flowers the first season. 2-3 feet.

### Note Our Terms On Page 1

PRICES, 25c EACH, $2.00 PER 10, $15.00 PER 100. NOTE EXCEPTIONS.

*Clump of Festiva Maxima Peonies.*

## Rudbeckia - Golden Glow

A yellow blooming perennial, that has become popular in a very short time since being introduced. The flowers in July and August are like small Chrysanthemums borne on the terminals of the 5-6 foot stalks. Very desirable. They are of the easiest culture, perfectly hardy and very free-blooming. One of the finest of all perennials.

## Shasta Daisies

Vigorous growing plants, height 2½-3 feet, simply masses of wonderful daisy-like flowers borne on great stems. They are fine for cutting for the house or mass effect in the border. No planting should be without them.

## Sweet Williams

Another good old-fashioned plant, so well known that description is not necessary. Flowers in June and is a picture with its white, violet and crimson blossoms. No old-fashioned border is complete without their cheerful, sweet-smelling and showy flowers. 18-24 inches.

## Tritoma - Red Hot Poker

This blooms from July until after frost time. The flower spikes are bright red cone-like heads that protrude above the drooping green leaves several feet. It is rather unusual and attractive. 2-3 feet.

They require protection during the winter, but are of very easy culture. For borders or massing on the lawn are very attractive. One of the most striking groups of plants in cultivation.

## Yucca - Adam's Needle

Y. Filamentosa (Adam's Needle or Thread Plant). A stately evergreen thread-leaved plant producing spikes of creamy white flowers, borne on tall stems. The individual flowers resemble the tube rose. Desirable to plant about a grave or wherever it may raise its majestic head in full array.

# Peonies

No other perennial compares favorably with the peony. It is so distinct, possessing many good qualities, that it is the standard of perfection. Ease of culture, hardiness, freedom from disease are qualities sought after and found in this grand old-fashioned flower. Like the oak, it seems to improve each succeeding year in size and beauty. The newer and improved varieties rival the rose in delicacy of color, fragrance and general beauty. No other large showy flower equals it singly, as a bouquet or for general decorative work. It thrives best in a deep, rich, sunny exposure, though does well in partial shade. A covering of leaves or manure each fall adds to its thriftiness. It may be used in the open border, along drives and walks, intermingled with shrubbery or other perennials, or in the background along the fence. We have spent much money and energy to collect the best and offer with confidence the following varieties in strong divided roots:

Prices, 50 cents each; $4.50 per 10; 12 different varieties, $5.00.

## White Peonies

**Festiva Maxima.** The grandest of the whites. Early. The flowers are extra large, color a pure white save carmine tipped petals. Has no equal.

**Coronne d'Or.** A cream colored white, compact blossom and very desirable. Late.

**Duke of Wellington.** A midseason white of unusual vigor, often having several blossoms to each stem.

**Mad. de Verneville.** Another very desirable white variety, free bloomer and should be in every collection.

## Red Peonies

**Francois Ortegat.** A midseason to late variety, being very dark rose color with yellow stamens; flowers large on strong stems. Extra good.

**Delachel.** A late deep rich red, of unusual color. An old favorite and esteemed by everyone that knows it.

**Felix Crousse.** A midseason variety of the most pleasing velvety red color, fading to lighter shades as the blossom falls.

## Pink Peonies

**Asa Gray.** A soft shell pink, mottled and veined rose. Midseason, and plant vigorous. Supply limited.

**Cayes (Duke of C).** An early deep rose, free bloomer and wonderful in bud.

**Alexander Dumas.** A strong midseason free-growing pink of deep and pleasing color.

**Faust.** This is an old favorite shell pink variety, midseason to late, a favorite with everyone that knows it.

**Fragrans.** Another deep rose of different season, valued for its fragrance and freedom with which it flowers.

**Humei.** The best late pink, American Beauty shade. Plants graceful and free flowering.

**La Tulipe.** Of later season, compact blossom, white with streaks of red and pink on many petals. Resembles the tulip somewhat.

**Margaret Girard.** Another delicate pink, midseason, of great vigor and size.

Evergreen Planting.

# Evergreens

Evergreens are a symbol of the never dying. They are able to adapt themselves to any type of soil, rocky, rich or poor, demanding pure air if expected to thrive. They are used principally in groups for best effect. For making vistas, wind breaks, contrast or character plantings, screens or to give variety, the evergreen is indispensable. More are planted every year and the supply has been limited for some seasons. We offer this season a fine lot of trees securely balled so as to insure safe transplanting. The soil should be rammed tightly about every root, or those planted without ball of earth should first have their roots dipped in thin mud. The broad leaved evergreens should be treated in this manner, and also clip off every leaf before planting.

Prices of evergreens include balling and burlapping—that is digging and shipping with soil about their roots. The pines make coarse root systems and we cannot dig satisfactorily with soil attached.

## Arbor-Vitae - Thuya

**Ellwanger's Arbor-Vitae** (T. Ellwangeriana). A compact form, pyramidal in habit with very finely cut foliage. Slightly bronzes in winter, the contrast being very effective.

2 feet ...............................$1.50

**Globe Arbor-Vitae** (T. globosa). A perfect globe when well grown, the spread usually equalling the height. Foliage of light green.

1½ feet .............................$1.50

**Hovey's Arbor-Vitae** (T. Hoveyi). Similar to above, of more rapid growth and lighter green. One of the best globular evergreens.

1½ feet .............................$1.25

**American Arbor-Vitae** (T. occidentalis). One of the most popular. These grow very kindly, will stand shearing like a hedge, being conical in habit of growth.

3-4 feet ...........................$1.50
4-5 feet ........................... 2.25

**Oriental Arbor-Vitae** (T. Orientalis). A striking color, pyramidal in shape and different from any of the other ones of this group.

3-4 feet ...........................$2.50

**Siberian Arbor-Vitae** (T. Wareana). A very dark green the entire year and for this reason most popular.

1½-2 feet ..........................$1.25
2-2½ feet .......................... 1.50

**Pyramidal Arbor-Vitae** (T. Pyramidalis). This is without doubt one of the very best cone-shaped evergreens known. Color a deep rich green, easy to transplant and if kept sheared will grow. 8-10 feet.

3-4 feet ...........................$2.00
4-5 feet ........................... 3.50

## Spruce - Picea

**Norway Spruce** (P. excelsa). A hedge of this variety will make an impenetrable barrier to trespassing, a wonderful enclosure for a lawn or garden, a windbreak for the residence, a fire protection from dangerous outbuildings, or planted on the lawn as specimens, or more especially in groups will prove most satisfactory. The tree is easy to transplant, grows rapidly and hasn't a fault. We offer this year some exceptionally well-shaped specimens—shipped with soil attached.

|  | Each |
|---|---|
| 5  -6   feet | $2.00 |
| 4½-5  feet | 1.50 |
| 4  -4½ feet | 1.25 |
| 3½-4   feet | 1.00 |
| 3  -3½ feet | .75 |
| 2  -2½ feet | .50 |
| 1½-2   feet | .45 |

**White Spruce** (P. alba). A very hardy evergreen, with deep green foliage, similar to Norway Spruce.

|  | Each |
|---|---|
| 1½-2   feet | $0.75 |
| 1  - 1½ feet | .60 |

**Koster's Blue Spruce** (P. pungens Kosteriana). A striking blue color, noticeable as far as can be seen. It may be used as a specimen or in roups with excellent effect. Very popular and deservedly so.

4 foot specimens .................$6.50 each

## The Pines - Pinus

**Austrian Pine** (P. Austriaca). A tall, massive, spreading tree, plumed with long, stiff, dark green needles. Useful for grouping or as a specimen.

| Not Balled | Each |
|---|---|
| 4½-5  feet | $1.50 |
| 4   -4½ feet | 1.25 |
| 3½-4   feet | 1.00 |

**Scotch Pine** (P. sylvestris). A strong, stiff growing variety with short green needles; more compact than Austrian Pine.

| | Each |
|---|---|
| 4   -4½ feet | $1.50 |
| 3½-4   feet | 1.25 |
| 3   -3½ feet | 1.00 |

**White Pine** (P. Strobus). This is perhaps the best of the pine family, being of rapid growth, pleasing color and easy to move.
2-2½ feet ........................$1.25

## Taxus - Yew

A dwarf growing evergreen, unusual with its bright green foliage. Needs some protection from hot sun and therefore valued for foundation work.
1½-2 feet .........................$1.50

## Boxwood - Buxus

**Handsworth Boxwood** (B. Handsworthii). An erect growing variety, with shining green leaves. Will stand pruning into any shape. Easy to transplant and will grow on any soil. For window boxes this is desirable.
18-24 inch plants ...................$0.60

## The Firs - Abies

**Nordmann's Fir** (A. Nordmanniana). Thick, dense tree of fine form; needles broad and dark green and lustrous. Silvery underneath.
3-4 feet ...........................$2.00
4-5 feet ........................... 3.00

**Douglas Fir** (A. Douglasii). A cone-shaped tree of very light bluish green foliage, even lighter on underneath side. Very desirable.
4-5 feet ...........................$2.50
3-4 feet ........................... 2.00

**Silver Fir** (A. concolor). This is a striking color, being a very light blue. Tree grows slowly, a perfect pyramid and if used with other evergreens the contrast in coloring is marked.
2-3 feet ...........................$2.50
1-2 feet ........................... 1.50

## Hemlocks - Tsuga

**Hemlock Spruce** (Tsuga canadensis). This is one of the most satisfactory evergreens known. A native and thrives on our soils. Can be sheared for hedges, or planted for windbreaks. Its graceful form and habit of growth make it valuable for planting in the foreground of heavy planting of Spruce, etc.
3-4 feet ...........................$2.50
2½-3 feet ........................... 1.75
2-2½ feet ........................... 1.50

## Mahonia

(See page 22).

## Juniper and Cedar - Juniperus

**Common Juniper** (J. Communis). A compact, columnar variety of unusual symmetry, except terminal branches which are slightly open. Somewhat similar to the Irish Juniper.
4-5 feet ...........................$2.50
5-6 feet ........................... 2.50

**Greek Juniper** (J. Excelsa Stricta). A dwarf pyramidal form, very compact, foliage bluish green
1½ feet ...........................$1.25

**Irish Juniper** (J. Hibernica). A slender, columnar form with glaucous green foliage. Used largely in formal work or in contrast with habit and color plantings. Needs no shearing.
5-6 feet ...........................$3.00
4-5 feet ........................... 2.50
3-4 feet ........................... 1.75
2-3 feet ........................... 1.00

**Pfitzeri's Juniper** (J. Pfitzeriana). Of the spreading types, this is perhaps the most popular. Foliage a grayish green, slightly drooping and branches are horizontally spreading.
1½-2 feet ...........................$1.50
2-2½ feet ........................... 2.00
2½-3 feet ........................... 3.00

**Prostrate Juniper** (J. Prostrata). Another trailing type that does well wherever planted. very satisfactory.
2-2½ feet ...........................$2.00

**Swedish Juniper** (J. Suecica). Resembles the Irish Juniper in erect habit of growth, the terminal of branches slightly drooping. Color, a grey green.
2  -2½ feet ...........................$1.50
1½-2  feet ........................... 1.25

**Savin's Juniper** (J. Sabina). One of the best. Spreading fan shape habit, of pleasing color of dark green. Stands the city dust, soot, etc., exceptionally well.
1½-2 feet ...........................$1.50

**Red Cedar** (J. Virginiana). A native tree, not half appreciated because of this fact. The nursery grown trees transplant more kindly than those dug from the hillsides. The tree is erect and of bluish green cast.
5-6 feet ...........................$3.50
4-5 feet ........................... 2.50

## Retinispora - Cypress

**Thread Branched Cypress** (R. filifera). Drooping string like branches of dark green. Habit rather conical.
1½-2 feet ...........................$2.00

**Golden Thread Branched Cypress** (R. filifera aurea). This is one of the best of the golden forms. Entire plant being of bright yellow color. Rather spreading in habit.
1½-2 feet ...........................$2.50

**Pea-fruited Cypress** (R. pisifera). Cone-shaped, foliage fine cut and rather drooping at tips. One of the best.
2½-3 feet ...........................$2.50

**Golden Pea-fruited Cypress** (R. pisifera aurea). Golden form of the preceding, tips of the branches being of bright yellow.
2-2½ feet ...........................$2.00
2½-3 feet ........................... 2.50

**Plumed Cypress** (R. plumosa). This is one of the best cone varieties. Foliage a grayish green, very finely cut and has a feathery appearance. Should be sheared during June or July.
2½-3 feet ...........................$2.00
3-4 feet ........................... 3.00

**Golden Plumed Cypress** (R. plumosa aurea). A golden form of the preceding, and very popular for foundation or group plantings.
2½-3 feet ...........................$2.50

**Veitch's Cypress** (R. squarrosa Veitchii). This is one of the best. Foliage a distinct bluish green, terminals silver. Very compact and rather semi-globe in habit of growth.
2-2½ feet ...........................$2.00
2½-3 feet ........................... 2.50

# INDEX

A. B. MORSE COMPANY, ST. JOSEPH, MICHIGAN

# BLUE GRASS NURSERIES

*H. F. Hillenmeyer & Sons*

## LEXINGTON,     KENTUCKY

CPSIA information can be obtained
at www.ICGtesting.com
Printed in the USA
BVHW081737201118
533619BV00008B/290/P